POSTCOLONIAL SPACE(S)

POSTCOLONIAL SPACE(S)

edited by
Gülsüm Baydar Nalbantoğlu
and
Wong Chong Thai

Princeton Architectural Press, New York

Published by
Princeton Architectural Press
37 East 7th Street
New York, New York 10003
212.995.9620

For a free catalog of books, call 1.800.722.6657
Visit our web site at www.papress.com

Library of Congress Cataloging-in-Publication Data
Postcolonial space(s) / edited by Gülsüm Baydar Nalbontoğlu
    and Wong Chong Thai.
        p.   cm.
    Includes bibliographical references.
    ISBN 1-56898-075-2 (alk. paper)
    1. Architecture and society. I. Nalbontoğlu, Gülsüm Baydar,
    1956– . II. Wong, Chong Thai, 1949– .
    NA2543.S6P67 1997
    720'.1'03—dc21   97-10109
                                                CIP

Introduction
Gülsüm Baydar Nalbantoğlu and Wong Chong Thai

The term "postcolonial space" is both a reminder of a colonial past and a salutary gesture towards the future. It conveys both a negative moment that displays and displaces binary constructions and fixed categories and a positive one of a promise of becoming for new languages, new subject positions, and new modes of spatiality. By using the term "space" rather than "architecture," we challenge the primacy of visuality that dominates contemporary architectural studies. Postcolonial space is a space of intervention into those architectural constructions that parade under a universalist guise and either exclude or repress differential spatialities of often disadvantaged ethnicities, communities, or peoples. This book, then, is an intervention into the disciplinary boundaries of architecture. It investigates questions of representation and interpretation, issues of difference and identity. It challenges regionalist positions that often frame studies on intercultural architectural encounters and that hardly question their own mechanisms of legitimacy.

Much work is yet to be done to open the margins of architectural knowledge and surface that has hitherto been silenced by disciplinary impositions. The essays in this book focus on postcolonial architectural encounters to explore such possibilities. Their aim, however, is neither to work "outside" the disciplinary boundaries of architecture nor to promote appreciation for hitherto unknown architectural cultures. The essays here are located at the interstices of a number of disciplines including architecture, literary theory, cultural studies, and philosophy. They are informed by poststructuralist theory, psychoanalytical interpretations, and feminist studies. On one hand they use specifically architectural vocabularies and address issues concerning current building practices, historical studies, and historiographical criticism. On the other hand they refuse to be contained by rigidly defined disciplinary frameworks and acknowledge that there can be no pure inside of architecture once its hegemonic assumptions—which are based on the primacy of vision, the autonomy of form, and the linear history of the master subject—are questioned.

As cultural critics like Gayatri Spivak and Homi Bhabha have emphasized, many familiar categories are blurred in postcolonial conditions. The multiple implications of hyphenated identities enter architectural discourse in a number of significant ways. East

and West, traditional and modern, marginal and central intersect and overlap in unprecedented and unexpected ways to produce new modes of spatiality and new architectural
expressions. The task of the postcolonial critic, however, cannot be to revalidate cultural
relativism and architectural pluralism. Any genuine attempt at the recognition of the other
calls for the questioning of the self. Critical studies of postcolonial spaces, which are
inscribed by differential identities, challenge perceptualist and formalist modes of
architectural writing and negotiate with the very concepts posited by architecture as its
"natural" epistemological grounds.

Postcolonial architectural discourse invariably engages with the
monumental binary constructions of East/West, traditional/modern, natural/cultural,
structural/ornamental, which prevailed in the discipline in the eighteenth century and are
perpetuated by contemporary regionalist positions. The proliferation of monographs and
architectural histories of non-Western cultures often bear testimony to a particular
construction of the other—which is informed by the cultural politics of colonial expansion.
A monolithic non-West is either de-privileged as irrational and pre-modern, or privileged
as the embodiment of values that are lost to the "enlightened" West. Oppositions like
mind/body and passive/active serve the purposes of the former position while spiritual/
material and natural/cultural belong to the latter. An ethnographic interest in the non-West
may expand the given boundaries of knowledge but does not transform it. While regionalist
positions are critical of the conventional hierarchies that privilege the modern over the
traditional and the international over the local, their interest lies more in finding a
reconciliatory middle term than in questioning the very systems of privilege. Postcolonial
positions, on the other hand, are interested in productive tensions arising from incommensurable differences rather than deceptive reconciliations.

A detailed critique of regionalism in its Western historical context is provided by Alan Colquhoun in his opening essay. There he explicates the founding premises
of the book by posing the critical question of the meaning and validity of regionalism today
when it is no longer possible to "correlate cultural codes with geographical regions."
Tracing the history of regionalism from the great modernist divide between rationalism and
romanticism to the rise of nativist and nationalist sentiments of the eighteenth and nineteenth centuries, he focuses on the intellectual responses to the increasing rationalization

of social life under industrial capitalism. Colquhoun states that regionalism as a search for an authentic cultural and architectural essence was formulated "precisely at the moment when the phenomena that it described seemed to be threatened and about to disappear." Since our only access to the "authentic thing" is by means of its later representations, any claim to regionalism is bound to remain a mimetic and reductive exercise. Colquhoun diagnoses that in the increasingly uniform and highly centralized cultural/political entities of the contemporary postindustrial world, the secure ground of regional differences is obliterated by "differences of an unpredictable, unstable, and apparently random kind." His concluding question is the starting point for the rest of the essays: "How should we define the kinds of architecture that are taking [regional architecture's] place?"

The major theme common to the following essays is the way in which difference and otherness inhabit architecture. They all recognize that such explorations have the power to alter the very terms by which conventional architectural discourses are stabilized. Each essay addresses the question from a specific angle and in relation to a particular architectural, cultural, historical, or historiographical context. Some focus on architectural expressions of alterity and cultural negotiation in a very material sense; others—recognizing that the repressed other can never be entirely contained in a given symbolic system—emphasize exclusions and specific mechanisms of repression. John Biln's study of Jean Nouvel's Arab World Institute and Vikramaditya Prakash's essay on Charles Correa's Jawahar Kala Kendra belong to the first category. Both are interested, though in different ways, in specific representational devices of architecture in producing critical effects that challenge the stability of given categories. Biln introduces the important issue of ethics, which is crucial in any discussion of otherness. Stating the impossibility of identifying some unified "authentic" other and of having access to any form of "radical alterity," he defines the site of interventionist struggle as "the site and mechanisms of our own self-serving constructions of the other." His reading of the Arab Institute is a self-consciously selective one where he emphasizes the critical use of Arab references that "are insistently marked as reflections of the West, rather than as truths of the East." By mixing and conflating the two voices of the "West" and "Arab" and hence disrupting self-privilege, Biln argues, the building not only demonstrates the inadequacies of the West's own mimicry of the Orient, but also suggests the existence of a radical otherness that is beyond articulation.

Prakash's essay follows Colquhoun's point that any claim to regional authenticity is bound to remain an endless exercise in mimetic representation. He argues that Charles Correa's mandala-inspired composition of Jawalal Kala Kendra suspends any question of an authentic Indian identity. At the interstices of Correa's writings on the topic and the architectural history and historiography of the mandala in India, Prakash traces a complex narrative of negotiations between Indian and Western architectural premises, the notions of center and margin, and the categories of universal and particular. He argues that the resulting reinterpretations have produced an endless series of historical transformations of the nine-square mandala that render the genesis of Jawahar Kala Kendra as an "after-the-fact, aesthetic transformation of the debris [of history], of which the original act is always already lost." Although he advocates the strategy of "re-covering" as a resistance to hegemonical cultural tendencies, Prakash ends his essay by a warning against the danger of "exemplification" in postcolonial critical acts.

Critical historiographical analysis lies at the core of Karen Burns's, Stephen Cairns's, and Gülsüm Baydar Nalbantoğlu's essays. In Burns's essay postcolonial space features as the space of architectural writing. She rethinks the terms by which notions of difference, identity, and architecture are addressed and questions criticism's effective modes of explanation. "Race" is the central theme in Burns's essay, which is both a historiographical critique and a reinterpretation of the house designed by Adolf Loos for the African-American dancer, Josephine Baker. The architectural writing that surrounds the house leads her to explore what is included in the history of architecture and what controls architecture's legitimate domains of reference. Burns argues that analyses of the Josephine Baker House, which stands for both racial difference and the difference of other discourses in architectural criticism, continuously gesture at but defer the issue of racial difference. Her questions on the production of Josephine Baker's subjectivity enable her to work with the friction of different discourses, including architectural criticism, cultural studies, and biography. Most importantly, perhaps, these questions and explorations lead to the active interruption of the legitimate domain of architectural discourse by establishing a close proximity to the issue of racial difference.

Cairns's and Nalbantoğlu's essays focus on the exclusions of the disciplinary boundaries of architecture. In an analysis of the colonial historiography of Java, Cairns surfaces the repression and exclusion of those architectural features that do not conform to the discipline's emphasis on a clear and unified expression of structure, function, and form. Focusing on the space of the *wayang* performances in the traditional Javanese house, he argues that the house has been excluded from both colonial and regionalist architectural agendas since its particular frame, screen, and shadow structure "operate outside the representational structure of the dichotomy between subject 'position' and object world." The flat, ornamental, and insubstantial nature of the *wayang*—almost dissolving form— opens a threatening space of radical alterity within the discipline of architecture.

Nalbantoğlu's essay explores the disciplinary limits of architecture in another context: the carved dwelling in the architectural discourse of modern Turkey. She explores the mechanisms by which the boundaries of the discipline are legitimized by violent acts of naming, assimilation, incorporation, and expulsion. These strategies are made possible, she argues, because of the exclusion of the notion of "lived spatiality" from architectural discourse, which is obsessed with formal studies. Her essay argues that recognitions of lived spatialities threaten *a priori* formal categories of architecture and surface irreconcilable tensions within its disciplinary boundaries.

The relationship between spatiality, language, and subjectivity is investigated in Mirjana Lozanovska's essay on the migrant house in Australia. Lozanovska argues that the boundaries between subject and object are blurred in the architecture of the migrant house, which she reads as the "site of the abject." Her essay explores how the mechanisms of abjection operate both culturally in relation to the hegemonic culture and individually in relation to the migrant identity. The "becoming" of female migrant subjectivities is the central concern of her analysis of the migrant house, which, she states, "is the spatial (pre)condition for the production of a different subjectivity, or rather a subjectivity in which difference proliferates."

The final essay by Wong Chong Thai refocuses the book on cross-cultural exchange at the global level. Wong claims that imaginary constructions of East and West are still dominant in contemporary critical studies where the East is rendered voiceless and left to be judged by an authority located elsewhere. His essay explores notions of incoherence, chaos, and randomness that are often associated with the architectural and urban spaces of the East. Using examples from a number of urban conditions, Wong states that in the metropolitan conditions of the East "all implications of some eternal future are deemphasized and replaced by an experimentation and invention for the here and now." His argument concludes that unprecedented historical and cultural connections and collusions in these spaces enable the subjects to move freely and "take flight into uncharted and unpredicted territories."

The range of arguments in this book are obviously not governed by one set of preconditions. They signal, however, that a predominantly Eurocentric architectural discourse that concentrates on transmissions of indigenous traditions is being challenged by studies on spatial negotiations across boundaries of culture, ethnicity, and gender. They alert us to the urgency to relocate and reinscribe the disciplinary priorities of function, form, and intention and focus on signification, spatiality, and legitimation. The recurrent themes of spatiality and subject formation, agency and legitimacy, the persistent attentiveness to unrepresented and unspoken architectural moments, and the implicit warning against the continuing effect of colonialism bear testimony to a common set of concerns, beliefs, and hopes voiced from the site of postcolonial architectural criticism.

The idea for this book was generated during an international conference, Architecture (post)Modernity and Difference, organized in Singapore in April 1993. The agenda was to initiate a forum to rethink contemporary architectural and urban conditions in the postcolonial world. The conference called for critical reexaminations of such binary constructs as West/non-West, globalization/regionalism, and center/margin in the context of postcolonial architectural cultures. During the event, an international group of architects, academics, and critics formed "Other Connections" as a loose collective to explore architectural and urban questions within the frames of postcolonial theory and criticism. The group decided to continue the Singapore forum at a second international meeting, Theaters of Decolonization: [Architecture] Agency [Urbanism], held in Chandigarh, India in January 1995. The aim of the second conference was to investigate the precise ways in which architecture and urbanism form and inform social and cultural interactions and identities. A third meeting Building, Dwelling, Drifting: Migrancy and the Limits of Architecture, is planned in June 1997 in Melbourne, Australia. Earlier versions of the essays in this book were presented in the first two forums.

The Concept of Regionalism
Alan Colquhoun

Ever since the late eighteenth century one of the main directions of architectural criticism has been that of regionalism. According to this approach, architecture
should be firmly based on specific regional practices based on climate, geography, local
materials, and local cultural traditions. It has been tacitly assumed that such a foundation is
necessary for the development of an authentic modern architecture. I want to subject this
idea itself to criticism and to consider the notion of regionalism so defined in relation to
the conditions of late capitalism.

I would like first to put the concept of regionalism into its historical context.
Let me begin, therefore, by looking at the historical period nearest to us, the avant-garde
of the early twentieth century. The twentieth-century avant-garde can always be viewed
from one of two perspectives: either as having inherited the principles of the Enlightenment, or as emerging from the tradition of the Enlightenment's great enemy, romanticism.
One can hardly avoid noticing the presence of these contradictory strands: on the one
hand the promotion of rationalism, universalism, and identity; on the other a recurrent
enthusiasm for nominalism, empiricism, intuition, and difference. These contradictions
came into the open during the famous debate between Hermann Muthesius and Henry
Van de Velde at the Deutsche Werkbund Conference at Cologne in 1914, when Van de
Velde maintained a Ruskinian belief in the virtues of the artist/craftsman and a betrayed
medieval tradition.

At first glance it would appear that the former stand—universalism and
rationalism—was triumphant in the Modern Movement of the 1920s. The elementariness
of de Stijl, the *rappel l'ordre* of Le Corbusier, and the *Neue Sachlichkeit* in Germany and
Switzerland were all basically rationalistic. But, as has often been pointed out, the situation
was in reality a good deal more complicated; rationalism was only one side of the Modern
Movement. For example, when the paradigm of Schinkelesque classicism emerged in the
first decade of the twentieth century, it not only laid claim to universal values but took over
and transformed the regionalist philosophy of the Art Nouveau movement that it replaced.
One example of this phenomenon is that classicism and "Mediterraneanism" were adopted

by the cultural nationalists of *Suisse romande*.[1] This fact was extremely influential in forming the mature ideology of Le Corbusier, in whose work reference to the Mediterranean vernacular (cubic form, white walls, etc.) was just as prominent as the idea of industrial standardization. These tendencies became increasingly important in Le Corbusier's work in the 1930s when, under the influence of anarcho-syndicalism, he began to think in terms of separate vernacular regional traditions, and even proposed a Europe divided into "natural" regions, including a Mediterranean region.[2] But Le Corbusier was only one case among many, though certainly the most articulate. Mediterraneanism was, I believe, deeply embedded in the whole Modern Movement from 1905 onwards. As for regionalism, one only has to look at the introductions to the successive editions of Sigfried Giedion's *Space, Time and Architecture*, first published in 1940 and revised in five editions until 1968, to realize the extent to which regionalist ideas increasingly permeated modernist theory in the post-World War II period. For example, Alvar Aalto's work was added in the second edition.

So there is a case for saying that the 1920s was not just the simple triumph of rationalism that it often seems. Instead, it should perhaps be seen as the stage on which a deep conflict of ideologies was still being enacted. What was the nature of this conflict? To answer this question it is necessary to go back to the eighteenth century and the beginnings of romanticism and historicism. It was then that Europeans started to notice the existence of ancient cultures that were neither antique nor Biblical. At the same time they began to be interested in their own pasts—in the vernaculars that had existed before the revival of antiquity in the Renaissance. One of the most significant results of this process was the creation of an alternative model for humanistic culture, one that made a sharp distinction between the study of nature and that of human history. Both Johann Gottfried Herder and Giambattista Vico independently claimed that the two studies demanded totally different methods, scientific in the one case and hermeneutic in the other.

This doctrine had a powerful effect in the German speaking countries because it coincided with the revolt against the hegemony of French culture. But it also affected France and England. Elaborate genealogies were invented to support the new sentiment of nationhood. The English traced their ancestry to the Anglo-Saxons, or, even more remotely, the Celts, who, in their Scottish Highland incarnation, arrived complete with a fictitious poet, Ossian. In Germany, the Goths were supposed to have invented

14

1. C.f. Guiliano Gresleri, "Vers une Architecture Classique," in Jacques Lacan, ed., *Le Corbusier, Une Encyclopedie* (Paris: Centre Georges Pompidou, 1987).
2. C.f. Mary McLeod, "Le Corbusier in Algiers," *Oppositions* 19/20 (Winter/Spring 1980): 55.

Gothic architecture on German soil until it was proved (by an Englishman) that this event had taken place on the Isle de France. I will return to this "invention of tradition," as it has been called by the historian Eric Hobsbawm,[3] when I come to mention the national romanticism of the late nineteenth century.

More important for an understanding of the origins of the doctrine of regionalism are the theories that were developed later in the nineteenth century, again mostly in Germany, concerning the problem of the rationalization of social life under industrial capitalism. This process was perhaps given its most powerful formulation by Max Weber when he coined two expressions that are still by-words for our present situation: the "disenchantment" of the world due to rationalization and secularization, and the "iron cage" of capitalism in which the modern world is imprisoned.

Among the concepts that German postromantic theory used, two are of particular interest, if only because they reduce the problem to simple binary oppositions. The first is the distinction between *Zivilization* and *Kultur*. As Norbert Elias has shown, this distinction goes back to the early nineteenth century and was the direct result of the German revolt against French cultural dominance. *Zivilization* meant aristocratic materialism and superficiality, as opposed to the less brilliant but more profound *Kultur*.[4] The idea of this distinction spread to other countries with the dissemination of romanticism. In England Samuel Taylor Coleridge adopted the word "culture" with its German connotations. The concept was absorbed by John Ruskin and William Morris, and, in the form of medievalism, became the cornerstone of the Arts and Crafts movement. In France itself, a school of historiography influenced by Chateaubriand held the view that the Frankish invasions of the fifth century were the true origins of modern French culture, rather than the institutions founded by the Gallo-Romans.[5] In the late nineteenth century the idea of *Zivilization* received the slightly different connotation of modern technological society, in opposition to preindustrial human values. But, both in the earlier and later senses, *Zivilization* represented the rational and universal as against the instinctual, autochthonous, and particular. We find approximately the same set of ideas in Giedion's *Space, Time and Architecture* when he talks about the split in modern life between feeling and intellect—a conflict that he hoped to dissolve by arguing that science and modern art were in reality dealing with the same phenomena but from different perspectives.

3. Eric Hobsbawm and Terence Ranger, ed., *The Invention of Tradition* (Cambridge: Cambridge University Press, 1983).
4. Norbert Elias, *History of Manners* (Oxford: Blackwell, 1994).
5. Martin Thom, "Tribes within Nations," in Homi Bhabha, ed., *Nation and Narration* (London: Routledge, 1990), 25–26.

The distinction between *Zivilization* and *Kultur* is a fruitful way of looking at the widespread nationalist movements of the 1890s, which in so many ways repeated the impulse of the earlier romantic movement. Just as the Germans had done around 1800, so a number of groups distanced themselves from the countries by which they had been politically or culturally dominated: the Irish from the English,[6] the Catalonians from the Castillians, the Finns from the Russians and the Swedes. In Finland, for example, the Finnish language was officially adopted,[7] an ancestral aural literature was "reconstructed," and an eclectic architecture representing "Finnishness" was put together from various stylistic sources, some indigenous, some external (for example, one of its main sources was the English Arts and Crafts movement). It need hardly be said that such a representation of national "essence" was largely fictional, but it had a clear ideological function: the legitimization of a nation-state in terms of a regional culture, and in this it was successful.

The notion of *Kultur* was taken up, in spirit if not in name, by chauvinistic movements in the late nineteenth and early twentieth centuries. Maurice Barres wrote in 1902,

> There is in France a state morality…Kantianism. This claims to regulate universal man, without taking individual differences into account. It tends to form young persons from Lorraine, Province, Brittany, and Paris in terms of an abstract, ideal man, who is everywhere the same, whereas the need will be for men rooted solidly in our soil, in our history.[8]

In Germany the idea was adopted by the National Socialists in the 1920s, taking up the ideas of writers like Houston Stewart Chamberlain, who had used the distinction *Zivilization/Kultur* to promote the concept of racial purity.[9] In so doing they recruited several architects of the *Heimatschutz* persuasion, such as Paul Schulze-Naumburg, whose ideas were derived from the Arts and Crafts movement.

The second concept I want to discuss is the distinction between *Gesell-schaft* and *Gemeinschaft*—a distinction made by Ferdinand Tönnies in his book of that title of 1887.[10] According to Tönnies these two words represent two types of human association. *Gesellschaft*-like associations are the result of rational deliberation, whereas *Gemeinschaft*-like associations are those that have developed organically. Again, we find the same opposition as in the case of *Zivilization* and *Kultur*, one term based on the idea of a natural

6. Though the Irish revolt started much earlier, its cultural manifestations belong to the 1890s.
7. As had already happened in the Balkans earlier in the century.
8. Maurice Barres, as cited in Thom, "Tribes within Nations," 38–39.
9. Houston Stewart Chamberlain, *Die Grundlagen des neunzehnten Jahrhunderts* (Munich: 1900). Translated into English as *Foundations of the Nineteenth Century* (New York: John Lane The Bodley Head, 1910).
10. Ferdinand Tönnies, *Gemeinschaft und Gesellschaft* (Leipzig: 1887).

law independent of historical or geographical contingency, the other implying rootedness in the soil. Examples of the former are bureaucracies, factories, and corporations, in which social relations are rational means to a desired end. Examples of the latter are the family, friendship groups, clans, and religious sects—all groupings in which social relations are ends in themselves.

I do not need to demonstrate that the doctrine of regionalism belongs to the *Kultur* and *Gemeinschaft* side of these oppositions. The problem I would like to address is this: given the radically changed circumstances of the modern world, does this cluster of concepts still make sense, and, if so, in what way will its culture—above all in its architectural manifestations—differ from those of its earlier incarnations: romanticism, Art Nouveau, and the early-twentieth-century avant-garde?

Obviously, the anxieties that were experienced in these periods have not simply evaporated. Many still feel disquiet at the increasingly abstract and homogenized world of modern postindustrial society. But it is questionable whether these doubts can any longer be expressed adequately in terms of the oppositions I have outlined. Clearly, the doctrine of regionalism is based on an ideal social model—one might call it the "essentialist model." According to this model, all societies contain a core, or essence, that must be discovered and preserved. One aspect of this essence lies in local geography, climate, and customs, involving the use and transformation of local, "natural" materials. This is the aspect that has most often been invoked in connection with architecture.

The first thing to note about this model is that it was formulated in the late eighteenth century precisely at the moment when the phenomena that it described seemed to be threatened and about to disappear. This is hardly surprising. The elements of society that operate without friction are invisible. It is only when imbalances and frictions begin to occur that it becomes possible to see them. So, from the start, the concept of a regional architecture was not exactly what it seemed. It was more an object of desire than one objective fact. That is why the architecture of regionalism put forward by the romantics could not be that "authentic thing" of which it had formed a mental image, but only its representation. The question as to whether such an "authentic thing" ever existed is an idle one, so long as our only access to it is by means of its later conceptualization. Nevertheless, the theory of regionalism adopted by the Modern Movement insisted on the need of such an architecture to be "authentic." Thus, what had to be eliminated were the very practices of the romantics themselves, by which *Gemeinschaft*-like societies had been invoked by mimicking their forms. It was not by such means that the essence of regional architectures could be recovered, but rather by discovering the causal relations that existed between forms and their environment. But if what I have said is correct this would be a hopeless task, even if we restricted ourselves to the regionalisms of romanticism. What would be discovered after the outer layer of mimetic forms had been removed would simply be a deeper level of mimesis. The use of local materials, sensitivity to context, scale, and so on would all be so many ways of representing "the idea" of an authentic, regional architecture. The search for absolute authenticity that the doctrine of regionalism implies is likely to create an oversimplified picture of a complex cultural situation.

Fear of such an oversimplified approach seems to have lain behind one of the more sophisticated recent theories of regionalism. By qualifying the old term "regionalism" with the new term "critical," Alexander Tzonis and Liane Lefaivre have tried to preempt any imputation of regressive nostalgia. According to them, the word "critical," in this context, means two things. First it means "resistance against the appropriation of a way of life and a bond of human relations by alien economic and power interests."[11] If we take away the mildly Marxian overtones of this statement what is left corresponds exactly to the notions of *Kultur* and *Gemeinschaft* that I have outlined above. It represents an attempt to preserve a regional essence that is seen to be in mortal danger and to uphold the qualities of *Kultur* against the incursions of a universalizing and rationalizing *Zivilization*. But any doctrine of regionalism has always implied such an intention, so that, taken in this sense, the word "critical" would seem to add nothing of substance to the concept. The second meaning Tzonis and Lefaivre give to the word "critical" is to create resistance against the merely nostalgic return of the past by removing regional elements from their natural contexts so as to defamiliarize them and create an effect of estrangement. This seems to be based on the Russian formalist theory of "making strange."

Now, these two meanings do not seem to have anything to do with each other. It seems that what is being presented as a single idea, "critical regionalism," is in fact two separate ideas. But the problem goes deeper, because the second interpretation of "critical" actually appears to contradict the first. It draws attention to the fact that the

11. Alexander Tzonis and Liane Lefaivre, "The Grid and the Pathway: An Introduction to the Work of Dimitris and Susana Antonakakis," *Architecture in Greece* 15 (Athens: 1981).

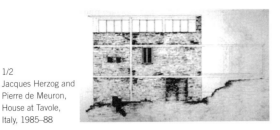

1/2
Jacques Herzog and
Pierre de Meuron,
House at Tavole,
Italy, 1985–88

postulated organic world of regional artifacts no longer exists. Far from resisting the appropriations of rationalization, it confirms them by suggesting that all that remains of an original, unitary body of regional architecture are shards, fragments, bits, and pieces that have been torn from their original context. Taking this view, any attempt to retrieve the original contents in all their original wholeness would result only in a sort of kitsch. The only possible attitude towards regionalism and the values of *Kultur* and *Gemeinschaft* would therefore be one of irony.

Behind the doctrine of a regionalism based on the old virtues of an organic (and therefore unconscious) social and artistic unity, there lies the doctrine of a sophisticated manneristic art that consciously juxtaposes incongruous elements to produce unstable combinations. This being so, perhaps we should stop using the word "regionalism" and look for other ways of conceptualizing the problems to which the word is supposed to respond. In saying this I am not saying that there are no longer any regions with their characteristic climates and customs. What I want to say is that regionality is only one among many concepts of architectural representation and that to give it special importance is to follow a well-trodden critical tradition that no longer has the relevance that it may have had in the past. It is true that many interesting contemporary designs refer to local materials, typologies, and morphologies. But in doing so their architects are not trying to express the essence of particular regions, but are using local features as motifs in a compositional process in order to produce original, unique, and context-relevant architectural ideas.

Take, for example, a recent building by the Swiss architects Jacques Herzog and Pierre de Meuron (figs. 1 and 2). In this small house in Italy there is play between local dry-stone walling (standing for the rural) and a "rational" concrete frame such that wall and frame are related in unexpected ways. It is impossible to read this building as a synthesis. Rather it is a sort of endless text. What we find here cannot be called "regionalism." Instead it is a work that makes subtle comments on a number of architectural codes, including the *fenêtre en longeur*, the cube, the frame, and the organicity of natural materials. One is not quite sure whether what is being suggested is tectonic solidity of theatricality, closure, or openness. In contemplating the building the mind tends to oscillate between a number of hypotheses, none of which are completely confirmed or denied.

3/4
Alvaro Siza, Housing in Schilderswijk, van der Vennestraat, The Hague, Netherlands, 1985–88

Another example is the housing recently built in The Hague, Netherlands, by Alvaro Siza (figs. 3 and 4). Here Siza imitates—but rather indirectly—certain features of Dutch vernacular classicism, such as its entry system, window proportions, and materials. Can this be called regionalism? If so, whose regionalism? But is not the question an absurdity? The one fact that could be called "regional" is its ownership. If one wants to use the word "regional" in such a context one must see it as a second-order system, filtered through the eclectic sensibility of a particular architect. It is the result of a voluntaristic interpretation of urbanistic values, one that takes into account existing urban forms as an artistic context; it is certainly not a confirmation of a living local tradition. The architectural codes that were once tied to the customs of autonomous cultural regions have long ago been liberated from this dependence. It is a matter of free choice. Localism and tradition-alism can therefore be seen as universal potentials always lurking on the reverse face of modernization and rationalization.

One of the intentions of a regionalist approach is the preservation of "difference." But difference, which used to be insured by the coexistence of water-tight and autonomous regions of culture, now depends largely on two other phenomena: individualism and the nation-state. As regards individualism, the architect, as the agent through which the work of architecture is realized, is himself the product of modern rationalization and division of labor. Designs that emphasize local architecture are no more privileged today than other ways of adapting architecture to the conditions of modernity. The combination of these various ways is the result of the choices of individual architects who are operating from within multiple codes.

In respect to the nation-state, in spite of the world-wide and almost instantaneous dissemination of technologies and codes, which results in an underlying similarity of the architecture in all Western and most Eastern countries at any one moment, it is usually possible to distinguish between the more typical products of individual countries. In a sense, the nation-state is the modern "region"—a region in which culture is coextensive with political power. But this culture is of a different kind from that of the regions of the preindustrial world. We may not quite agree with Ernst Renan when, in a lecture at the Sorbonne in 1882, he denied that national boundaries were dictated by language, race, religion, or any other "natural" factor.[12] But at least we can admit the truth

12. Ernst Renan, as cited in Homi Bhabha, "Dissemination: Time, Narrative and the Margins of the Modern Nation," in Bhabha, *Nation and Narration*, 310.

of his statement that what creates a nation is a will towards political unity rather than any preexistent set of customs. These two functions may be coextensive but they do not have to be. The need for placing regions that often differ from each other under a single political umbrella comes from the needs of the modern industrial economy. As Ernest Gellner has pointed out, the reasons for the rise of the nation-state were the opposite of those underlying regional differentiation. Differences between regions were part of the structure of the agrarian world. The needs of industrial society, on the contrary, demand a high degree of uniformity and the flattening out of local differences.[13]

Perhaps it will be argued that this is not true universally. Recent events in the ex-Yugoslavia and the ex-USSR have shown that old regional identities are still very much alive. But it is difficult to assess the status of regionalism in these cases, since it is obvious that ethnic emotions are being fanned for political reasons—that is, reasons connected with the formation of modern nation-states and the control of political power. The conflict in the ex-Yugoslavia cannot be attributed to profound differences in regional cultures but rather to residues of previous conflicts between the Hapsburg, Ottoman, and Russian empires. As far as architecture and everyday artifacts are concerned, the cultures of the combatants are identical. The person who stands for the satanic "other" is not marked by any specific cultural differences. Indeed one of the striking aspects of the television coverage of the war is that it is taking place in the familiar and banal context of badly built modern blocks of apartments and supermarkets—contexts common to the entire modern world.

A more plausible exception may be made of the so-called "developing world"—especially that part of the third world consisting of ancient cultures, such as the Indian and the Islamic. In these countries, it will be argued, nationhood does sometimes coincide with living cultural traditions—traditions that are in conflict with modernization. But however much we hope that crucial aspects of these traditions may turn out to be conformable with modernization, we have to admit that the modern technologies and cultural paradigms that increasingly predominate in the urban centers of these countries also affect the rural areas. In these societies, different historical times exist together, and under these circumstances it is already difficult to speak of "authentic" local traditions in a cultural field such as architecture. It may be desirable to satisfy the demand for traditional

13. Ernest Gellner, *Nations and Nationalism* (Oxford: Basil Blackwell, 1983), chapter 7.

forms with their socially embedded, allegorical meanings, even though the artistic and craftsmanlike traditions that originally supported them have begun to atrophy, due to prolonged contact with the West. But these are matters of strategy rather than of essence.

With these questions we come to the core of the problem. What is the relation between cultural patterns and technologies? The problem is, to some extent, obscured in the West, because industrialization evolved out of local cultural traditions, and adaptation to a postindustrialized culture is already quite far advanced. The problem is glaring, however, in the East and in Africa because of the friction between two worlds and two times: the agrarian and the industrial. Are cultural patterns absolutely dependent on an industrial base, or can they maintain a certain independence? Is an industrialized culture irrevocably Eurocentric?

But these questions take me too far from my theme, and I would like to end by looking again at the problem from the point of view of the technologically advanced countries, and at the same time to sum up my observations on the concept of regionalism, as it concerns these countries. Modern postindustrial culture is more uniform than traditional cultures because the means of production and dissemination are standardized and ubiquitous. But this uniformity seems to be compensated for by a flexibility that comes from the nature of modern techniques of communication, making it possible to move rapidly between codes and to vary messages to an unprecedented extent. This greater freedom, this ability of industrial society to tolerate difference within itself, however, does not follow the same laws that accounted for differences within traditional societies. In these societies, codes within a given cultural region were completely rigid. It was precisely this rigidity that accounted for the differences between different regions. In modern societies these regional differences are largely obliterated. Instead, there exist large, uniform, highly centralized cultural/political entities, within which differences of an unpredictable, unstable, and apparently random kind tend to develop.

The concept of regionality depends on it being possible to correlate cultural codes with geographical regions. It is based on traditional systems of communication in which climate, geography, craft traditions, and religions are absolutely determining. These determinants are rapidly disappearing and in large parts of the world no longer exist. That being the case, how is "value" established? Whereas in earlier times value belonged to the world of necessity, it now belongs to the world of freedom that Immanuel Kant foretold at the end of the eighteenth century. Modern society is polyvalent—that is to say, its codes are generated randomly from within a universal system of rationalization that, in itself, claims to be "value free."

Clearly this way of generating meaning and difference in modern technological society has serious consequences for architecture, whose codes have always been even less amenable to individual and random manipulation than the other "arts" and more dependent on impersonal and imperative typologies and techniques. In the preindustrialized world these technologies—summed up in the Greek word *techne*—were connected with myths relating to the earth and the cosmos. In modern society "technique" is irreversibly disconnected from the phenomenal world of the visible, tangible experience upon which such myths were built. In the modern media the process of means-end abstraction has resulted in the rerouting of artistic codes from the stable to the apparently random. To speak more accurately, they have been rerouted from the public to the private realm. Such a process of "privatization" was suggested by Michel de Certeau, for whom modern technocratic life has not so much destroyed the myths and narratives characteristic of agrarian societies, as it has confined them to the family and the individual, where they reappear as fragments of an older narration.[14]

This, then, is the problem of architecture in the postmodern world. It seems no longer possible to envisage an architecture that has the stable, public meanings that it had when it was connected with the soil and with the regions. How should we define the kinds of architecture that are taking its place?

14. Michel de Certeau, *The Practice of Everyday Life* (Berkeley: University of California Press, 1984).

(De)forming Self and Other: Toward an Ethics of Distance
John Biln

Introduction: Partial Unraveling

The Arab World Institute Building by Jean Nouvel is generally acknowledged to occupy an important position among recent works of architecture. Although there
is no question that its technical competence is extraordinary and that its poetic command of
modernist and of "high-tech" styles is excellent, this building is significant for several reasons
beyond those usually offered. The value of the project goes beyond its considerable interest
as a "postcolonial" commission. Central among its strengths is the way that it reveals an
architectural condition I will call "ethical." Certainly, political and ethical issues have been
raised in other contemporary works, but unlike the Arab Institute many of these projects
have the rhetorical advantage of remaining purposefully marginal, unbuildable, or wholly
investigative in intent. Surprisingly, perhaps, the power of this project derives precisely from
its difficult status as a built and occupied work. It effectively seeks to affirm its architectural
"utility" at the same time that it works critically on its programmatic and symbolic charges.

As we know, aesthetic works often function at one moment, or in one way,
to produce certain effects, and then may seem to work at other moments against themselves to disrupt or displace these same effects. Such works may operate in very complex
and subtle ways only to arrive at some contradictory or self-defeating end.[1] Yet under
analysis it can occasionally be demonstrated that this end is more or less consistent,
perhaps even in some sense "inevitable." Among such works might be counted a few of
those that directly challenge or raise difficult questions about that body of unnoticed,
invisible, or sedimentary notions that circumscribe what "counts" as the acceptable, the
preferable, the desirable, and the possible. Projects of this type implicitly raise the question
of just how "ethical" or "political" an architectural work can be. Nouvel's Arab Institute
brings these issues forward in a very public way.

Of particular interest in this context are Nouvel's reflections on the various
modes of representation present in and around the architectural work.[2] In the Arab
Institute project, these reflections amount to a critique of that institute's mission of
representing the Arab world to the West. It should be clear that when I speak about

1. For a particularly clear expression of this notion in the context of deconstructive criticism, see
Gayatri Chakravorty Spivak, "Translator's Preface" to Jacques Derrida, *Of Grammatology* (Baltimore:
Johns Hopkins University Press, 1976).

2. In the present essay, when reference is made to the architect "Nouvel," this is generally meant to
signify the assembly of architects involved in the design of the project. It is well known that Jean
Nouvel tends to favor collaborative ventures over individual work, and unless the reference is to a
statement made directly by Nouvel himself, his name is used as shorthand for this collaboration.
However, even Nouvel's personal comments on the building have been fragmentary and contradictory.
Citations to Jean Nouvel are only to those of his statements that seem appropriate to the partial
reading of the Arab Institute undertaken here. Assuming one were interested in some more inclusive

1
West wall, book
tower: form and
reflection

architecture in these terms, that is, when I speak about a self-imposed architectural criticism of Western constructions of the other, I am most obviously speaking about built form itself, rather than, or only, about architectural "narrative."[3] I will show that Nouvel's work broadly addresses the "self-other" relationship as constructed in and through architecture, and, further, that Nouvel's work explores specific strategies for using architectural devices of representation against the grain to produce what might be called "self-distancing" effects.

Much of the following discussion is descriptive of the Arab Institute. Although the term "description" is often taken to suggest some sort of even-handed treatment, the following reflections are decidedly schematic, incomplete, and openly "partial." Indeed, since the focus here is upon only those several features of the work that seem relevant to issues of the East this treatment of the Arab Institute is highly foreshortened and one-sided.[4] However, it would be a mistake to suppose that this suggests a consciously critical or resolutely negative approach. The following reading of Nouvel's work is purposefully "affirmative" in the sense that it attempts to assert and ratify one particular moment in the work while it ignores or brackets others. This partial view of the work reflects a belief that there is something important in the building, something perhaps so fragile and tentative that a certain benefit of the doubt is necessary in order that it be seen at all (fig. 1).

On Task: Rendering Delirious

It is clear that discussions of "self" and "other" can take many general forms. From the point of view of the so-called "Western intellectual," the problem is fraught with a number of difficulties, not the least of which involves the ambiguous demand to somehow allow the voice of the other to emerge. A number of writers have pointed out the difficulties involved in actually doing this. If nothing else, it is naive to listen for any single, unified voice; that is, it is surely impossible to identify some simply "authentic" other. Perhaps Jacques Derrida's strategy of "rendering delirious" or Julia Kristeva's "putting on trial" our *own* self-induced constructions of the other are among the least intrusive approaches. This is what Gayatri Spivak has suggested in her discussions of the postcolonial woman as "subaltern."[5] Spivak notes that fundamental to Derrida's critical project is the explicit notion that self-constructed "centering" is a double move. While

26   project, it would still be difficult to extract any "definitive" position from the comments Nouvel has
made, let alone to construct a position that unified the voices of the other designers involved.
3. In the context of the formal reading of the building undertaken here, comments about what the
Arab Institute "indicates" or "intends" refer to the implied voice and tone of the work. This articulation is rooted in the forms and contexts of the building, rather than in any "real" author. It does not
necessarily coincide with the intentions of any of the architects involved. Although uses of the names
"Nouvel" and "Arab Institute" are intended to help keep the writing as simple as possible, tactics of
this kind significantly compromise precision and rigor in the process. Issues of this type involving
authorship and control are exceedingly complex and beyond the scope of the present discussion.
4. In any case, this approach is not antithetical to at least one intention for the building. Apparently in

concealing the necessity and inevitability of a submerged "second" or oppositional term (to which a privileged first term owes its existence), this "other," locked as it is in a closed discourse of sameness or self-presence, is itself inescapably never more than an assimilation of a necessarily and radically disjunctive other. Any such centering produces an "other" that is both secondary and under-privileged (with regards to a privileged "first" term) and appropriative and supersessive (with regards to some radically disjunctive other). This second and parallel moment in centering, this displacement of an "external" other or radical alterity, is insurmountable. Any assertion of equivalence between these two "others" serves only to conceal the rift between them.

For Spivak, this understanding of closure to otherness within discourse suggests certain possibilities for application to the analysis of intentional impulses within a work. Spivak accepts Pierre Macherey's proposition that what a work does not say, is, for the work of literature, perhaps indeed what it cannot say.[6] However, for collective ideology (specifically, for Spivak, the codifying legal practices of imperialism), that which the work does not say may be more usefully understood as what it refuses to say. Once inability is reconceptualized, under certain conditions, as refusal, appropriative practices are opened to conscious political and critical intervention. For Spivak, the critical task becomes one of de-privileging the disciplinary discourse where it relies on a self-serving definition of otherness that sublates a fundamentally unknowable *tout autre chose*. It is here that Derrida's call for a "rendering delirious [of] that interior voice that is the other in us"[7] can be seen to converge with the political project of ideological de-privileging. Although Spivak is interested in using deconstruction for institutional self-criticism, her point that the ideological moment is fundamentally a self-serving refusal of otherness applies to understanding works of architecture. This approach is based on a recognition that radical otherness is inherently unknowable, and that the site of interventionist struggle is therefore more properly the site and mechanisms of our own self-serving constructions of the other. Ultimately, such constructions do violence both to ourselves and to all others.

On Topos: Other Constructions

Nouvel's Arab Institute Building houses the Arab World Institute's operations in Paris, symbolically and materially supporting the institute's charge of promoting

a reference to Clifford Geertz, Nouvel has commented that "[Robert] Venturi talks about complexity, I talk about thickness. I'd like to think that the [Arab Institute] can sustain many different investigations, interrogations, observations, from near or far, and that the detail reinforces the whole." See Patrice Goulet, *Jean Nouvel* (Paris: Electa, 1987), 40. Translation courtesy Thomas Hartman.

5. Gayatri Chakravorty Spivak, "Can the Subaltern Speak?," in *Marxism and the Interpretation of Culture* (Chicago: University of Illinois Press, 1988).

6. See Pierre Macherey, *A Theory of Literary Production* (London: Routledge, 1978).

7. The translation that appears in Spivak's article differs slightly from John Leavey, Jr.'s, the more recent translation of Derrida's text. Leavey's revised translation of the passage in question is as follows: "The overlordly tone dominates and is dominated by the oracular voice that covers over the

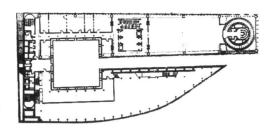

2
Fourth floor plan:
hollow center

France's "knowledge and understanding of the Arab world, language, civilization, and dynamic development." The institute's mission is to "encourage cultural exchanges, communication, and cooperation between France and the Arab world, particularly in the fields of science and technology." The institute is also supposed to "play an active role in the development of relations between France, Europe, and the Arab world."[8]

According to Nouvel's published statements, the building program includes a library and documentation center, a museum of Arab art and civilization, a gallery for contemporary Arab arts and crafts, an auditorium, and a number of assembly rooms and offices.[9] In reality, the building also houses a cafeteria and restaurant services, parking facilities, and other ancillary functions. Nouvel's selective rendering of the program already indicates something of the value Nouvel places on certain of the program elements. And Nouvel's privileging of parts of the program does rather accurately identify the thrust of the institute's operations. These almost exclusively involve various forms of representation. The building houses program elements supporting textual and documentary representation (the library), material culture and figural representation (the museum and the gallery), verbal and visual representation (the auditorium), as well as whatever services (parking facilities and other ancillary functions) Nouvel's representation might utilize. The building effectively supports a reductive metonymic operation in which a variety of "Arab" objects, images, and discourses are substituted for the multiform density of a lived experience of Arab culture(s).

Nouvel has commented that the design of the building "takes into account, in dialectical terms," a series of dualities. Among these are the "Arab" and the "Western" (referring to the work's cultural contexts), the "traditional" and the "modern" (referring to the work's urban contexts), "history" and "modernity" (referring to the work's time), and "interiority" and "openness" (referring to the work's formal configuration).[10] According to Daralice Boles, these "dichotomies … are revealed and then resolved" in the design, with the architects uncovering "the underlying affinity between Modern and Arabian architecture, [and] shaping connections between the two at the abstract level of space and geometry."[11] In a sense this is true, but it misses something important about the work. The building does point out the dialectical relationships between these various pairs, and it does reduce their apparent differences to an abstract identity in "space and geometry." But

28

voice of reason, rather parasitizes it, causes it to derail or become delirious. To raise the tone, in this case, is to make it jump, is to make the inner voice delirious, the inner voice of the other in us." Refer to Jacques Derrida, "On a Newly Arisen Apocalyptic Tone in Philosophy," trans. John Leavey, Jr., in Peter Fenves, ed., *Raising the Tone in Philosophy: Late Essays by Immanuel Kant, Transformative Critique by Jacques Derrida* (Baltimore: Johns Hopkins University Press, 1993), 131.

8. Jean Nouvel and Hubert Tonka, *Institut du Monde Arabe: Une Architecture de Jean Nouvel, Gilbert Lezénés, Pierre Soria, Architecture Studio* (Paris: Éditions du Demi-Cercle, 1990), 58.

9. Ibid.

10. Ibid.

11. Daralice Boles, "Modernism in the City," *Progressive Architecture* 7 (1987): 72.

3
Patio: Arab Institute
and Notre Dame,
correspondence and
incommensurability

apparently this is because Nouvel recognizes that whatever the "Arab" is, it will remain out of the grasp of his architecture, that any dualities presented in the work will always remain within the interpretive economy of the West. As Nouvel points out, the work's "symbolism and modernity are rooted in present-day interpretations of the history of these two civilizations."[12] That is, Nouvel appears to be more interested in interrogating the West than in attempting to grasp some elusive "truth" elsewhere. He has commented that his interest in architecture proceeds from a desire to question the relationship between built work and the cultural context in which it is produced:

> For me, architecture is the introduction of cultural values of civilization and sensitivity in what has been constructed: what is there in what has been constructed compared to that in our civilization? How can we recognize it as an acquisitive part of civilization.[13]

Nouvel makes explicit reference to the traditional *mushrabiyya* in the high-tech screen wall on the south end of the Arab Institute, and he reproduces something like an Arabian enclosed court at the deepest point in the plan. Nouvel notes other "Arab" forms in the project, as well. However, he is always careful to draw attention to just this reduction of the "other" to the "same." It is worth remembering here that the French, in particular, have a long-standing and abiding interest in so-called "Arabian" culture, and have very literally made it their own through heavily invested interpretations and repetitions of tales, stories, and images of the "Orient." In the French colonies indigenous culture was everywhere thoroughly and radically altered by French influence. The most obvious symptom of this is the profound and persistent use of the French language at all levels of French colonial society, but the influence obviously goes far beyond language. However, even if it were somehow possible to understand the terms "Arab" and "Western" as labels for relatively autonomous and culturally distinct systems of representation, each system would still be capable only of reducing to some form of identity the heterogeneous subjects they seek to "represent" (figs. 2 and 3).

In the founding gesture of the formal partis, the visual and axial relationships between the enclosed court (reminiscent of past Arab forms) and the apse of Notre Dame (Gothic and Christian), Nouvel suggests both the obvious correspondence and the apparent incommensurability of these two elements. On the one hand, they manifestly share a single

12. Nouvel and Tonka, *Institut du Monde Arabe*, 58.
13. Jean Nouvel, "Potentiality and Present," in Josep Lluis Mateo, ed., *Jean Nouvel, La Obra Reciente 1987–1990* (Barcelona: Quaderns d'Arquitectura I Urbanisme, 1989), 32.

4
Screen wall:
two traditions,
one economy

cultural economy, remaining within practices and discourses of the West: both are products of Western authors, both use materials and techniques in their times paradigmatic of the West, both are installed in the center of the same Western capital, both serve the same cultural community, and so on. On the other hand, they appear quite different: the court is within the building, the apse without; the court is secular, the apse sacred; the court is open, the apse closed; the court is circumstantial, the apse essential; and so on (fig. 4).

However, this production of "difference" is just another form of reduction, one in which the "same" is quietly installed as identity-in-opposition. The Arab Institute implicitly acknowledges and exposes its inability to preserve within itself any difference-as-alterity: instead of reducing difference to a simple identity, instead of naively constructing something more literally "Arab" and "other," Nouvel produces from difference a dichotomy that is at once an inscription of the same and a knowing critique of that same inscription. Examples of this abound. Arab references are insistently marked as reflections of the West, rather than as truths of the East. This is apparent even in the tectonics of the building. In the celebrated south wall, for example, the traditional, integral, static, and passive *mushrabiyya* is appropriated, fragmented, technologized, activated, and recomposed as an assembly of distinctly Western building "components." These metal diaphragms are part of a system that actively monitors and hydraulically controls various aperture sizes to respond both to broad seasonal cycles and to momentary temporal changes. They work as high-tech componentry at the same time that they make formal gestures to their Arab "origins."

Nouvel has made it clear that the building is to be understood first in visual terms. He has made numerous references to the various views afforded by the architecture, the extreme transparency of the work, the modulations of its light, the qualities of its reflections, and so on. And it is initially through "vision" that Nouvel produces what can be understood as a radical critique of the representational function of the building. The building evidences an awareness that representation-in-metonymy is a powerful and insidious form of resolution that flattens a heterogeneous life-world to a comfortable understanding. The building further suggests that the problem is not to be solved by some better, some more complete, some more adequate representation. The Arab Institute reveals an implicit understanding that representation-in-metonymy is incomplete not because the institution can accommodate only a portion of all its cultural

5/6/7
Museum: conflation
and condensation;
distortion, fusing,
impurity; embodied
seeing and a
disembodied view

representations, but rather because representation itself is always partial: it always and necessarily both misses what cannot be represented and misrepresents what can.

Nouvel has summarized the building as "Technology...put to purposes other than its own representation. In certain parts of the Arab World Institute, layers that are eighty meters apart appear superimposed. When I watch the setting sun through the book tower, I tell myself we have created a truly transparent building."[14] Although in this passage Nouvel is referring to the "poetic" functions of technology (or tectonics) in the work, he has also said that architecture "must speak, relate, question, if necessary in detriment (and it often is) to technological purity, to constructed tradition, to conformity with references to cultural models.... [C]ritical, provocative, denouncing, interrogating, ironic stances must be adopted."[15] In commenting on his interest in exploring the "limits of the possible," Nouvel has also noted that it is "impossible to push reality forward unless existing conventions in the act of constructing, the latent protocol between the architect and society, are also given a push."[16]

In fact, there does seem to be a critical edge to the building's "transparency" (figs. 5 and 6). Museum spaces are usually conceived of as support environments in which the objects on display have primary importance. The north-facing galleries in the Arab Institute, however, suggest a different and much more critical strategy. Certainly the protection, maintenance, and display of the collection is materially enabled in Nouvel's building, but at the same time any passive and uncritical contemplation of these objects is disrupted by a proliferation of the visual. The display cases, conventionally furniture-like third elements between the displayed (Arab) object and the (Western) building, work here to compress, conflate, and condense the two. The materials of the cases are uncompromisingly those of the building, while their function is aligned with the objects they contain. But the extreme transparency and reflectivity of the display cases works against any visually definitive separation of contained object from containing architecture, related artifact from unrelated one, central space from peripheral space (fig. 7).

Almost nowhere in the gallery are the museum collections isolated and free from the "impurities" of visual interference. The representations of Arab culture—the objects, images, artifacts, and texts that "stand in" for the (absent) culture—are always seen highly mediated by reflections, superimpositions, layerings, distortions, and fusings

14. Jean Nouvel, cited in Marie Christine Loriers, "Through the Looking Glass," *Progressive Architecture* 5 (1988): 94.
15. Jean Nouvel, "The Future of Architecture is Not Architectural," in Mateo, *Jean Nouvel*, 124.
16. Jean Nouvel, "Tactics and Strategies," interview with Bea Goller, in Mateo, *Jean Nouvel*, 124.

of other images and views "properly" considered external, peripheral, unrelated, or contradictory to those pieces on display. Curatorial narratives are everywhere displaced or disrupted. Every sighting is compromised, every view haunted by the unexpected and disruptive presence of other views, alternative images, additional representations. The "Arab" is never given by itself. And neither is the building; neither the gallery, the architecture, the site, the city context—the "West," within and without. The serigraphs of Paris reproduced on the glass facade facing the old city across the Seine make explicit and rhetorical a strategy that is otherwise implicit and experiential in the gallery spaces. Superimposed on a single glass surface, given fully and immediately, are both the ghost representations of the old city and the direct or "real" images available to perception. This mutual and multiple contamination of a singular sight has the effect, first, of visually disrupting any notion of the simple substitution of Arab or Western representation for some absent represented (while avoiding the temptation to seek the "truth" of the represented), and, second, of casting doubt on the possibility of discovering the Arab other within the Western building's own economy of the same (while avoiding the temptation to suppose that the other is "simply" the same). Nouvel's project seems resolutely self-critical, skeptical of representation but convinced of its necessity, locked in the same but in pursuit of self-difference.

Architectural commentators have made much of the directly felt "sensual" power of the Arab Institute Building.[17] The emphasis Nouvel places on the visual suggests that larger phenomenal possibilities of sight in the project should not be dismissed out of hand. Indeed, Nouvel has noted that part of the architect's cultural responsibility involves a subversion grounded both in vision and in sensation: "Subversiveness is produced when the nature of architecture in terms of the production of *images* and *sensations* raises doubts about social conventions and produces reactions of fear in the economic field."[18] In fact, in the Arab Institute a conventionally static and disembodied "view" repeatedly opens onto an active and embodied "seeing."[19] In the north gallery spaces, for example, the interpenetration of views is not choreographed to produce a singular narrative. Even very slight movements on the gallery visitor's part produce unpredictable visual effects, in part because a visitor's physical movement puts into play necessarily disconnected but synchronic effects of reflection and transparency. While movements that might stabilize

17. For a poetic rendering of this view, see Hubert Tonka, "Impressions d'Oeuvre," in Nouvel and Tonka, *Institut du Monde Arabe*, 2–8.
18. Nouvel, "Tactics and Strategies," 126; emphasis added.
19. For a discussion of "seeing" and "viewing," see John A. Schumacher, *Human Posture: The Nature of Inquiry* (Albany: State University of New York Press, 1989), especially 64–67.

8
Ninth floor hall:
punctuation of
movement

layered views can be contrived by a visitor, reflections constituting a different system continually escape this control (fig. 8).

In other areas of the building similar awarenesses of movement are provoked visually. On the stairs in the entrance lobby and in the library tower, small vertical or spiral movements generate a wide variety of overlaid interior and exterior views. In areas where walls of translucent marble panels define space (in the patio and cafeteria areas, primarily), views "through" are produced only by way of deliberate body positioning in which the eyes must be aligned with gaps between panels in order to see anything at all. The variety of opening sizes and the temporal "volatility" of the south screen wall diaphragms demand carefully positioning one's body to frame or extend selected views of the city; in many of the areas along the south wall, strong patterns of light and shadow rhythmically punctuate movement through space and reinforce a sense of physical embodiment.

On Tone: Ends Without End

These visual strategies gesture toward a suspension of belief in the transparency of representation, and toward a felt sense of viewer embodiment. A privileging of the visual in the Arab Institute has the paradoxical effects of actively heightening awareness of the extra-visual, of experientially questioning ideological notions of the Arab other, and of casting doubt upon the general and usually implicit truth claimed by representation itself. The nature of these effects, grounded as they are in the physical co-presence of viewer and building, suggest that whatever "ethical" or "political" work the Arab Institute performs, such work is constrained to some local de-privileging of Western ideologies of the other. Acknowledging the rootedness of architecture, it would seem that these operations are largely directed toward, and the effects largely received by, the institute's "own" community.[20] And the internal logic of the project, involving a displacement of Western identity-in-opposition rather than a search for some "real" Arab other, suggests that the project's self-inscribed field of operation is indeed the ideologically local.

This self-displacement relies on the tone of the work rather than on its style. Obviously, there are any number of ways to utilize "high-tech" components, "modern" forms, or "Arab" references. In the Arab Institute, signs and symbols of "self"

20. Notwithstanding the building's secondary effects within the various circuits of publication and promotion.

and "other" are always presented together but at a distance from the work itself, within the work but not as the work. Even as the work "speaks" the construction of self and other, the site of this speech is complex, doubled, distanced. The project recognizes that its provenance is Western, but it does so without collapsing this recognition into a simple identification with the West; as I have shown, the project puts the "Arab" into play as well. The project mixes and conflates two voices, each originating at the same site, each commonly original; the Arab Institute articulates the "other" as self-spoken. As Derrida notes, "To change voice or mimic the intonation of the other, one must be able to confuse or induce a confusion between two voices, two voices of the other and, necessarily, of the other in oneself."[21] The project has no real access to some radically exterior other. Nonetheless, in its demonstration of how the West's "own" mimicry of the Orient can only fall short, the project suggests the existence of some absolutely disjunctive other. It repeatedly gestures toward this other other—an other beyond reach, outside the West's self-referential economy, finally beyond articulation.

In its invocation of an other beyond itself, the Arab Institute mirrors both a general condition and a possibility of discourse. Derrida suggests that all such formulation is apocalyptic in the sense that, even as it claims "truth" and "closure," it is finally unfounded. That is, all discourse, all representation, relies on an absolute it cannot supply, a certitude that remains questionable. The "stable" ground of all claims to adequate representation necessarily lies outside the place and moment of the speech that asserts it, located in an unreachable other-ness beyond itself. As we have seen, the Arab Institute invokes other voices, multiple intrusions, unexpected conflations and juxtapositions. Derrida points out that in such a situation no one knows *who* is speaking. And without knowing who speaks, there is no ground, no anchor, no finality that can convincingly underwrite the spoken. This implies that it is futile to listen for some "voice of the other." Arrival, closure, or final certification will always remain forestalled, forever beyond its announcement. For Derrida, all that can be done is to try to "hear with the ear of the other," that is, to hear of and with an other condition forever delayed, radically exterior, always to come, and never present. And as Peter Fenves notes, "To hear with, and along with, the ear of the other is to hear the tone of the apocalypse . . . it is never itself but is always, if only virtually, another."[22] In the Arab Institute, we are able to sense an *other*

34

21. Derrida, "Newly Arisen Tone," 129.
22. Peter Fenves, "The Topicality of Tone," in Fenves, *Raising the Tone*, 38.

apocalypse, an apocalyptic interruption of the unveiling/unmasking presumed present in representation (where, finally, what is unveiled is always already limited to the self-constructed). To hear with the ear of the other, and, for us, to hear along with the Arab Institute, is to hear what only another-to-come can hear, to put oneself on guard against what oneself only can say.

The Arab Institute's apocalyptic tone announces not the West's own other, but the delayed eventuality of an other "to come," an other that will never arrive. Peter Fenves points out that it is precisely "the ineluctable plurality of languages and voices [that] gives rise to the topic of tone." This plurality "is not a mere aggregate of homogeneous languages or voices, each of which would derive from the same source." Instead, it ushers in a heterogeneity, and rhetoric of astonishment "incommensurable with the language of measurement, schematization, counting, cognition, and representational thought in general."[23] In the Arab Institute, this tonal intrusion is accompanied by and accomplished with a bodily motion activated explicitly outside (or alongside) the representations upon which such motion casts doubt. The movement-of-the-same established by the discourse between the West and its "Arab" other is repeatedly frustrated and exposed in the lived and living actions orchestrated by the Arab Institute Building. Invisible seams in the norm are pulled apart. The trajectories of representation are altered. And here, quite as Derrida suggests, "By its very tone, the mixing of voices, genres, and codes, apocalyptic discourse can also, in dislocating destinations, dismantle the dominant contract or concordat."[24] In the Arab Institute, ideologies otherwise taken as stable and reliable are shaken to the core.

Nouvel puts into play both registers of Derrida's apocalyptic tonality: both destination (truth) and derailment (truth's interruption). The Arab Institute Building is actively marked by a distance, a self-silencing, a listening that refuses closure in representation. And this disruptive posture is suggested to occupants by way of an embodiment that appeals to the concrete particularity of the lived body, to an order of existence outside (or alongside) the representations offered in the building. This is, above all, an invitation to hold open preconceptions of other, and, finally, preconceptions of self. Fenves reminds us that the term "tone" "has undertaken the task of designating an insensible—unmeasurable if not immense—dimension of discourse." As such, it "traverses the cleft separating the sensible from the intelligible."[25] It is precisely this cleft that the

35   23. Ibid., 8.
24. Jacques Derrida, "Newly Arisen Tone," 160.
25. Fenves, "Topicality of Tone," 11.

Arab Institute holds open for us. Indeed, Nouvel plays upon the openness of architecture itself, its weakness, its lack of control over practice(s), its fragile representations. By remaining silent, by provoking sensate movement in occupants, Nouvel acknowledges and utilizes this constitutive weakness of architecture. The apparent (and only apparent) "finality" of built form and museological narrative is used in the Arab Institute as an "authoritative" terrain upon which to open onto disruption and instability that presumed revelation of truth insisted upon by Western "certitude." The Arab Institute moves to unsettle settlement itself.

This movement is necessarily mobile, never finished, and never conclusive. It lies beyond the architecture that provokes it. As we have seen, its locus is the *experience* of the building rather than the building itself. This suggests something like Jacques Ranciere's "subjectivization," the "formation of a one that is not a self but is the relation of a self to an other,"[26] the production of the self as "outsider" or "in-between." In the Arab Institute, fixed representations are frozen and exposed as the individual undertakes a movement always both physical and conceptual. At the same time, these representations are themselves put into play, along with the lived self, as materials for remaking the self-other contract. We have seen, however, that the Arab Institute suggests that another other, some radical alterity, always lies beyond reach. This can only have the effect of casting doubt upon any such remaking. We are thus constantly returned to the unstable zone between identity-formations, neither able to reassume a comfortable self nor able to find quiescence somewhere certain beyond the self.

Michel de Certeau has written that ethics (in the sense of "ethos," a way of being) "is articulated through effective operations [defining] a distance between what is and what ought to be," a distance designating "a space where we have something to do."[27] On this view, the Arab Institute is strictly "ethical." It disrupts self-privilege and opens a space for doubt that can be filled only with some mobile reconception of the self-other relationship. This can only be accomplished in, through, and as a destabilization of those self-conceptions founded upon reflected "images" of the other. But de Certeau's "ought to be" may well be undoing itself. Thus, even as some reworking may finally take a previous (or new) form of self-privilege, the Arab Institute insistently demands that some "space to do" be reopened in the lived experience of the work.

26. Jacques Ranciere, "Politics, Identification, and Subjectivization," *October* 61 (Summer 1992): 61.
27. Michel de Certeau, "History: Science and Fiction," in *Heterologies: Discourse on the Other* (Minneapolis: University of Minnesota Press, 1986), 199.

Indeed, the project demands we recognize at least some possibility of holding open this space, indefinitely suspending or deferring the closure of representation. This may well be a self-absorbed strategy; perhaps in this it is again all too Western. But it might also serve as a caution for the so-called "colonized," and not just for the "colonizer." Even if generalizing and unifying postcolonial counter-constructions of identity are politically effective in resisting a history of imposed colonial constructions, a resolutely self-critical stance may be crucial here as well, lest resistance turn into reaction, difference into essence, and, more to the point, lest emancipatory postcolonialism turn toward some repressive form of neo-nativism. We need to open ourselves not to what we are, but rather to what we might be and to what we might become. Indeed, the Arab Institute serves as a reminder to us all that a strategy of self-disruption may finally hold the most promise for ushering in that fragile silence without which any whispers of self-becoming, and any voice of the other, will always and only be presumed heard.

Identity Production in Postcolonial Indian Architecture: Re-Covering What We Never Had
Vikramaditya Prakash

Stories of origin are far more telling of their time of telling, than of the time they claim to tell.—Robin Evans

When one talks of an Indian architect, or of an architect from the "non-Western" world, it seems necessary to deal with the question of identity. While discussing Western architects one can get away with dealing with supposedly universal architectural issues like aesthetics and technology, but it seems necessary that in discussing the work of an architect from India the issue of identity be specifically raised in addition to, or in dialogue with, issues more directly aesthetic or architectural. Architects of the West do not specifically make Western buildings. Architects of the non-West are expected to. Even architects of the West working in the non-West in one way or another find themselves obliged to deal with the issue of non-Western identity.

The question of origin underlies any claim to identity. However, simple recovery of the unmediated or unspoiled essence is not the usual stated goal of commentary on contemporary Indian architecture. Rather, it is the phrase "modern Indian" that is the critical password and evaluative touchstone of such commentaries. It is something of an oxymoron because while "Indian" is an identity claim that in some way or other inevitably relies on a backward look to the past or a beginning, "modern" signifies the simultaneous desire for a telescoped rush into the future, freed from a dragging anchoring in the past. The immense power of suggestion that the phrase exerts, then, must be an effect precisely of its sense of compression of seeming opposites.

In 1984, in the preface to a monograph, Bombay-based architect Charles Correa affects this compression as follows:

> We live in countries of great cultural heritage. Countries which wear their past as easily as a woman drapes her sari. But in understanding and using this past, let us never forget the actual living conditions of many of the peoples of Asia, and their desperate struggle to shape a better future. Only

a decadent architecture looks obsessively backward ("I have seen the past and it works.") At its most vital, architecture is an agent of change. To invent tomorrow; that is its finest function.[1]

Correa's academic and aesthetic affiliations are originally locatable in the canons of Western modern architecture. Building on the "sari" metaphor, one can interpret Correa's image of the past draped around an "India" as the habitual, custom-prompted response of a supine "feminine" India. A few years later, however, Correa attributed to this femininity the strength of a certain resilience that remained untouched by the massive public "interventions in the fields of law, administration, transport, and communication" brought about by Western colonists. Although the colonists also brought with them the new myths of science, rationalism, and progress, Correa argues that the "vast majority [of them] were soldiers or administrators or traders, and to assert their presence (or perhaps to reassure themselves) they imported European architecture and lifestyles to the subcontinent, regardless of any relevance they might have had." He continues,

> Architecture based on the superficial transfer of images from another culture or another age cannot survive; architecture must be generated from the *transformation* of those images, that is by expressing anew the mythic beliefs that underlie those images.[2]

Transformation and not transfer, thus, is the crucial evaluative distinction that discriminates between claims of successful negotiations between the past and the future of "modern India." Transformation, Correa asserts, is an act of reinvention, that "places architecture where it rightfully belongs: at the intersection of culture, technology, and human aspiration."[3] How does one know if a work is able to "express anew mythic beliefs" and not fall victim to the "superficial transfer of images"? What are the contours of this transaction? And why is this transaction inevitably policed by the uniformed figure of the "West"?

In addressing these questions I am interested in the manner in which aesthetic or formal constructions inscribe and are inscribed by the more discursive or language-based frameworks of identity. This is in good part a question of evaluation, and evaluating aesthetic works is always a perilous business. There is no guarantee of a tight fit between the discursive frameworks of language and ethics and the more sensory impressions

1. Charles Correa cited in Sherban Cantacuzino, *Charles Correa* (Singapore: Mimar, 1984), preface.
2. Charles Correa, "The Public, The Private and the Sacred," *Architecture + Design*, vol. 8, no. 5 (1991): 91–99, emphasis in the original.
3. Ibid., 96.

of form and aesthetics. What is good and right is not necessarily beautiful. Architects, one might argue, are supposed to be judged by their buildings and not by their writings; they are expected to be fundamentally visual people, not literary. Yet writing to "explain" an aesthetic work—that strictly by definition should be precisely "unexplainable"—is the unbridled urge, all disclaimers notwithstanding, of not only critics and historians but architects themselves. Words execute a powerful hold on our imagination. As a consequence, more often than not, an architectural work that may be very complex and multilayered in itself becomes so closely aligned with its "official explanation" that it is difficult to interpret it differently. This, of course, need not always be the case, but it becomes unavoidable when one is dealing with a building that comes with an "explanation" supplied by the architect, making the task of critical commentary more difficult, or easier, depending on your point of view.

The case at hand is Charles Correa's design for the Jawahar Kala Kendra in Jaipur, India, a state-sponsored institution devoted to the preservation and promotion of traditional arts and crafts. The Kendra's plan, as proffered by the architect, is derived from one of the cosmic diagrams of Hindu mythology—the nine square "mandala." Mandalas not only govern the astrological plans of Hindu temples but describe the structure of the universe, as given in some of the ancient mythological texts of Hinduism. ("Mandalas," according to Correa, are square diagrams subdivided symmetrically about the center, creating series of 4, 9, 16, 25 . . . up to 1,024. Though it forms the basis of architecture, the "mandala," Correa explains, "is not a plan; it represents an energy field" that "explains the true nature of the cosmos."[4]) I am not a scholar of religion, and it is not the purpose of this essay to evaluate and judge the validity of Correa's interpretation of the mandalas. Using the mandala as nothing more, but nothing less, than one of the constituent threads of the Kendra's weave, I am interested in unfolding some of the ways in which architects use aesthetic devices that, more than shining with exemplary brilliance in the light of their official explanations, harbor illuminating insights (however subdued) of their own— especially those that might help expose hidden blind spots of the former. In the following, thus, I will argue that Correa's Kendra does a lot more, and not less, than Correa claims it does. My argument necessarily will be somewhat circuitous, and in the process I will engage some of the other threads of the network that make contemporary Indian architecture "Indian" and "modern."

4. Correa, "Public, Private and Sacred," 92.

1
Charles Correa,
Jawahar Kala
Kendra, Jaipur, plan

2
Le Corbusier,
Governor's Palace,
Chandigarh, plan

Identity and Recognition:
Jawahar Kala Kendra and the Nine-Square Mandala

Jawahar Kala Kendra is based on a partitioned nine-square plan forming a self-enclosed object that is encased in high walls (fig. 1). Viewed through the formal logic of plan forms, the Kendra is an excellent case study in the "nine-square problem." As John Hejduk has pointed out, the productive contradiction in the nine-square problem is that it simultaneously affords complete fluidity (drawn up as a grid of sixteen points) and complete containment (as network of interlocking partitions placed on grid lines).[5]

While Hejduk's Texas houses explore the characteristics of both possibilities, it is no doubt Le Corbusier's innumerable explorations of the free plan, interweaving the domino grid, explore and exploit this contradiction in some of the most forceful ways. A useful comparison can be made between Le Corbusier's plans of the unbuilt Governor's Palace in Chandigarh and that of Correa's Kendra. As was his kilt, Le Corbusier placed a grid of sixteen columns forming a nine-square grid well within a surrounding envelope (fig. 2). Anchored around the regulating authority of this grid of columns, the plans of the Governor's Palace form a tense but stable equilibrium of essentially equivalent interlocking spaces. With the envelope remaining firm, the internal walls flow according to sensuous curves, occasionally intersecting with, but more often bleeding past, the columns. Indeed the tension between the rhythmic columns and the walls that tend to slide by is crucial to the composition.

Ignoring the displaced entrance square for the moment, Correa's Kendra, by contrast, is defined by load-bearing walls that run on the grid lines, giving rise to a pattern of distinct adjacent squares. Effectively exploiting its large size, the impending fragmentation of the plan into nine self-contained squares is offset by a network of corridors that link adjacent squares and distribute circulation around the building. Unlike the composition of the Governor's Palace, where the circulation core in the center is in no other sense more significant that the spaces that connect to it, that of the Kendra crucially relies on the dominant open-to-sky presence of the central square that has axial openings into the circulating corridors. The result is a distinctly hierarchical plan in which the relatively even flow of interlocking corridor spaces is punctuated on axis by long vistas across the central square. The Kendra's play between interlocking spaces and distinct vistas

5. John Hejduk, *The Mask of Medusa* (New York: Rizzoli, 1985), 37–38.

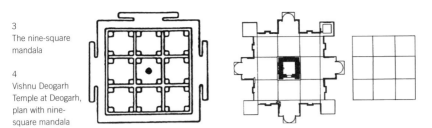

3
The nine-square mandala

4
Vishnu Deogarh Temple at Deogarh, plan with nine-square mandala

has the most unexpected consequence: though overarching in their regulating presence, the eight interlocked squares of the Kendra's plan seem to disappear in the criss-cross of visual axes that shoot through its fabric. Thus, instead of acting as containers of distinct spatial experiences, the Kendra's walls become the generating medium of a schizophrenic duality—potentially a much more complex, albeit schizoid, arrangement than that of the Governor's Palace.

Now, I would have liked to have led this discussion towards the different subjectivities of the imagined users precipitated by the two plans—one more idealized, unified, and symmetrical and the other more complex and fragmentary. But I could be accused of straying far afield because Le Corbusier's "spatial pyrotechnics" (to use Correa's apt phrase) is not the stated "origin" of Correa's design. Rather, as we know, the Kendra's plan is supposed to be a transformation of the mandala, specifically the nine-square mandala. Claiming origin in a mandala, of course, lends the Kendra a much more recognizable "Indian" identity claim than one that I might have been able to produce through the elaborate stage sets of projective formal identifications. At an immediate level it is quite easy to see the correspondence between a nine-square mandala and the nine-square Kendra plan—they both have nine squares (fig. 3). In what way, then, is the Kendra a transformation, and not a case of simple transfer, of the mandala?

Hindu temples are based on mandalas, but the relation between the mandalas and the actual plans of temples is that of approximation. If the mandalas give the ideal, unmanifest order of the cosmos, the temples are particularized, manifest embodiments of mandalas, constructed as approximations of that ideal order. As material manifestations of an order that must by definition remain ideal, the plans of the temples are derived by geometric displacements that ensure that the walls of the temple precisely do *not* occupy the ideal geometry of the mandala—but only approximate it by literally cutting corners.[6] Elaborate developments of such "corner cutting" give the fantastic stepped plans of north Indian Hindu temples. The basic idea can be illustrated by the way the walls of the Vishnu Temple at Deogarh slide past and beyond the grid of the nine-square mandala on which they are based[7] (fig. 4). (Indeed, by this logic it is Le Corbusier's plan for the Governor's Palace that transforms the rule of the mandala, and not that of Correa's Kendra.)

6. For a complete discussion see Andreas Volwahsen, *Living Architecture: India* (New York: Grosset and Dunlap, 1971).
7. This example in fact comes from an essay that is in the same issue of *Architecture + Design* that has a reprint of Correa's "The Public, The Private and the Sacred." See Madhu Khanna, "Space, Time and Nature in Indian Architecture," *Architecture + Design*, vol. 8, no. 5 (1991): 51–64.

Yet I would hesitate to criticize Correa's invocation of the mandala as "outside the rule." To evaluate the "authenticity" of a derivation on the basis of strict fidelity to claimed precedents is to validate a univalent logic of identity that works through the establishment of correspondence, devaluing difference. In a different register, then, one can note that the correspondence between temples and mandalas is far more difficult to *recognize* than that between the Kendra's plan and its mandala. The Kendra's plan is *recognizably* more like that of a mandala than that of the temples, even though it is precisely the latter that are supposed to be "truly" based on the mandalas. For the uninitiated urban reader of today this *recognizability*, of course, would be crucial.

If one uses recognition as the key, however, one necessarily has to deal with the discursive, socially constituted systems of signification—language and history—as part of the interpretive framework of the Kendra. That language recognition is important is in fact suggested by Correa's use on the walls of symbols that—like Robert Venturi's billboards—identify the built work by naming it. Naming as a system of producing identity functions through the recognition of correspondence and differences between signs. The sign "cat" functions through its identity with other signs "cat" and through its difference from other "non-cat" signs. Signs weave together to generate meaning through eternally deferring networks that produce contingent, contextualized "meaning effects." Extracting meaning, then, involves the active work of interpretive reading using the received frameworks of history. Here the author's intentionality is only one of the interpretive frameworks.

What, then, might the Kendra's plan as the reinvention of a nine-square mandala mean, from this point of view? Needless to say, the following reading is as much a product of my interests as of those suggested by the Kendra and Correa. It must be evaluated as much for its own claims as for its fidelity to that of the Kendra's primary reading, that is, that of Correa.

Identity in the Discursive Frameworks of History: Colonial and Postcolonial

At one level of interpretation, the Kendra's plan and formal characteristics are those of Venturi's "billboard"—they are oversized, up for display, and easily readable, with a simple message. Without in any sense self-consciously attempting to interact with the complexities of Indian history or with processes of cultural transformation, Correa's Kendra satisfies an impatient media-trained sensibility. It is a very photogenic building that indeed seems to be designed for the camera. Seemingly plucked from the lavish catalogues of the pundits of "traditional" Indian culture, the identifiable stereotypical "Indian" elements—like *jharokhas* (broken step formations) and Jain cosmological and Tantric paintings that grace the courts and walls of the Kendra—suggest the elaborate stage sets of a Hindi film studio.

At another level, however, it is possible to trace a more complex narrative. For this, we have to make a detour through some of the contexts that frame Correa's work as a postcolonial artist.[8] Correa's opening lines of the essay that I have been quoting, that is, "The Public, the Private and the Sacred," resurrect a world view that is generally associated with Plato:

> We live in a world of manifest phenomena. Yet, since the beginning of time, man has intuitively sensed the existence of another world: a nonmanifest world whose presence underlies—and makes endurable—the one he experiences everyday.[9]

That the essential Hindu philosophy believes that the manifest world is simply *maya* or illusion and it is the purpose of aesthetics to disclose the nonmanifest is an idea that has now run an amazingly consistent course from the discoveries of the "enlightened" colonists of the late nineteenth century, through the writings of many Indian nationalists, right down to the clichéd introduction of a basic tourist guide to India. Early proponents of this neo-Platonic interpretation, formalists like E. B. Havell and Ananda K. Coomaraswamy, for instance, opposed the mid-nineteenth-century colonial claim that Indian art and architecture was valuable only as mere ornamentation.[10] They promoted new interpretations to lay claim to equivalent philosophical foundations underlying Indian art and architecture as legitimate responses against the claimed superiority of Western aesthetics. As "enlightened" colonists, they took upon themselves the task of determining an appropriate architecture for India. They went on the search for examples that were deemed to be "truly Indian" and "not of decayed" character. Since they were strongly influenced by the Arts and Crafts Movement and its fetishized memory of a lost medieval crafts tradition, it is not surprising to find that what they considered "truly Indian" was

8. Language and vision are closely related but irreducibly different. As architects work, the translation between the two usually tends to privilege one or the other; either building forms are offered as "embodiments" of ideas, or ideas are proffered as explanations of building forms. I attempt to bring the two into contestable dialogue. In traveling the highway between them I am, needless to say, driven by my own interests and desires, and accordingly my text does not claim to speak for or take the place of either the architect or the building. Textually, here I weave my agency in much the same way that I believe Correa's design remakes "Indian" identity—not by claimed faithfulness to an origin, but by its reinterpretation motivated by my own contingencies and demands.

9. Correa, "Public, Private and Sacred," 91.

10. For a detailed analysis see Tapati Guha-Thakorte, *The Making of an New "Indian" Art: Artists,*

what was produced in the spirit of the medieval craftsmen of Europe, of which India was considered a living embodiment. What they considered "not of decayed" character was what was not excessively ornamental or, more importantly, not influenced by European architecture. Thus, by projecting onto the native craftsman their own fantasy of a lost origin (medieval Europe) and by producing him as a pure "other," the "enlightened" colonist could vicariously, through the fantasy of a recovered lost origin, produce his own pure identity as the "other" of the "other," that is, the pure European or Westerner. In the nineteenth century, architectural discourse was used thus to appropriate the margin to fix the center.[11]

In what seems like a repetition with little change, there has been a renewal of interest in traditional or vernacular space and culture over the last twenty-five years or so, in the wake of the disintegration of what might be termed the internationalism of modern architecture. The motivating impulse of the contemporary re-renewal of interest in Indian identity is the displacement of the equivalent claims of Eurocentric modern archi-tecture in India—represented chiefly by the legacies of Le Corbusier and Louis Kahn.[12]

As a person committed to self-determination, I must, of course, support such "regional" architecture as voices from the hitherto-suppressed margins. But, centralizing the margins remains a risky enterprise, whether it is done in the name of multiculturalism or decolonization. For the limited success of centering regional identities, the risk run by these "non-Western" architects, is their habilitation as the representative tokens of the margins. Working in the name of, but against the long-term interests of, decolonization, these architects can be effectively re-marginalized by being cast as the margins of a global culture whose center remains a mythologized West. How, then, can one claim marginality without, precisely, becoming the dutiful margin of a re-centralized, neocolonial world? How is one to negotiate and assert difference in an affirmative way that is not a simple reversal of the colonial?

In both the nineteenth century and now, the crucial evaluation revolved around the claimed "authenticity" of the architect's interpretation of cultural identity or roots or origins. But there are specific differences in the colonial and contemporary efforts in their material manifestation. An instructive comparison can be made between a colonial institution and Correa's "postcolonial" Kendra. After India came directly under the Crown

 Aesthetics and Nationalism in Bengal, c. 1850–1920 (Cambridge: Cambridge University Press, 1992).
11. See Vikramaditya Prakash, "Productions of Identity in (Post)Colonial 'Indian' Architecture: Hege-mony and its Discontents in Nineteenth-Century Jaipur" (Ph.D. dissertation, Cornell University, 1994).
12. Of the many examples of literature on this subject, see especially V. Bhatt and Peter Scriver, *After the Masters: Contemporary Indian Architecture* (Ahmadabad: Mapin Publishing, 1987).

5
Swinton Jacob,
Albert Hall

6
Albert Hall, urban
locational plan

in 1858, "modern" schools of art, exhibitions, portfolios of architectural details, measured drawings, and, quintessentially, museums were pressed into service to resurrect and legitimize "correct" interpretations of "Indian" architecture. North of Correa's Kendra, just outside the walls of the old city of Jaipur, there stands a late-nineteenth-century museum called Albert Hall, designed to preserve and promote the arts and crafts that were perceived to be dying due to the corrupting influence of England and due to lack of patronage. The building itself was constructed as an instructive museum, with details from various buildings from around the country reconstructed in it. But these details remained precisely that—details—and were made demonstrably subservient to the overall formal symmetry and functional distribution of the design (figs. 5 and 6). These were carefully controlled by the British engineer-turned-architect, Swinton Jacob. Unified by a Western formal aesthetic, Albert Hall can be interpreted as a condensation of the ideology of "empire" in which colonial hegemony is legitimized by the subsumption of all differences under the universal sanction of "empire."[13]

If Albert Hall signified itself as a centralized order whose universality was signified by its extension into infinity (the model of object in space), Jawahar Kala Kendra signified itself as a decentralized order whose claims to universality are signified, precisely, by a contained universality (the model of the enclosed object as container of a universal ideal). The former had to cover up and subsume difference in its all-encompassing munificence. The latter had to specifically produce difference, which then was legitimized by its claims to universality and thereby subsumed the universal. The particular cannot be simply particular.

To subtend itself as a particular order—organized around a central square that is its access to universality—the Kendra utilizes the visual, aesthetic device of a beginning boundary (which is also its limiting edge). This it does by cordoning itself off from the continuity of the rest of the world. With visual recognition as the key, the Kendra can be identified with the walled cities of India, that, even more than mandalas, are recognizable visual icons of Indian identity. It is important to note that the enclosed-wall cities of India became symbols of a closed, self-absorbed, mysterious, static (and unhygienic) conception of Indian society *after* the colonists had started building outside these cities using the diametrically opposed formal composition device—the object in

13. I have argued this at much greater length in my Ph.D. dissertation "Productions of Identity in (Post)Colonial 'Indian' Architecture: Hegemony and its Discontents in Nineteenth-Century Jaipur." The political function of this enterprise was to speak for the native; re-presentation (as in art and philosophy) acted in the service of representation (as in speaking for). It functioned, in other words, to rob the native of his (potentially subversive) autonomous agency and to locate this agency, instead, under the umbrella of "empire." That was what made the colonial architecture hegemonic, rather than its supposed "inability" to grasp the "Indian ethos."

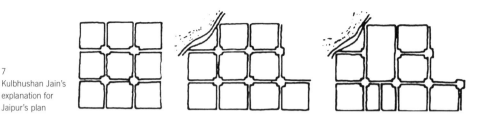

7
Kulbhushan Jain's
explanation for
Jaipur's plan

space. Now Jawahar Kala Kendra (like numerous other projects intent on resurrecting the lost glories of the walled city) must first delineate itself an ideal space, carved out off the general space that is identified as non-Indian or Western. In the nineteenth century the marginal was up for grabs to fix the center. Now the marginal must first produce itself as marginal to negotiate with the center.

Identity and Agency:
"Aesthetic Insight" and the Contingencies of the Particular

Correa's plan for the Kendra contains a very specific reference to the old city of Jaipur. One of the examples highlighted by Correa to illustrate "transformation" is Sawai Jai Singh's making of Jaipur. For the colonists Jaipur's ascription to ancient planning principles was simply a means of inscribing "native" identity within the stereotype.[14] In 1978 Kulbhushan Jain, a professor of the School of Architecture, Ahmadabad, proposed a new inscription. The plan of Jaipur, Jain postulated, was significant not only because it was based on one of the mandalas (Jain suggested the nine-square mandala) but more importantly because in practice it embodied a secular adaptation of the underlying cosmic principle. The nine-square plan of Jaipur, Jain suggested, could not be laid out as the ideal type because the northwest corner ran into the Nahargarh hills. So, Jain argued, Sawai Jai Singh must have simply shifted that square diagonally across and relocated it at the edge of the lower southeastern one[15] (fig. 7). Jain's reinscription was closely tied into human agency as the mediating and transforming act between sacred and secular, ideal and adaptation, theory and practice.

In this diagonal relocation, Jain located the principle that describes human agency. According to Jain, in the making of Jaipur the human was manifested as an aesthetic response to the "manifest" world. This aesthetic response was a formal act that both signified and constituted this agency, as the latter mediated between the manifest and the "nonmanifest."

This is how Correa describes the aesthetic insight of S. Jai Singh, prefiguring his own work of two and a half centuries later:

> Maharaja Jai Singh, who founded the city, was also a renowned astronomer. . . . In the planning of Jaipur, he embarked on a truly

14. That the plan of Jaipur is based on ancient Shastraic text was first promoted by T. H. Hendley in the commemorative volumes of the 1883 Jaipur Exhibition. He suggested that the plan seems to have been based on a "Prastara" type plan. This was one of the ideal city plan types that had been listed by Ram Raz in his *Essay on the Architecture of the Hindoos* (Varanasi: Indological Book House, reprint 1972).
15. Kulbhushan Jain, "Morphostructure of a Planned City, Jaipur India," *Architecture + Urbanism* (August 1978): 107–20.

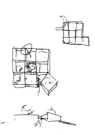

8
Charles Correa's
conceptual sketch
of Jawahar Kala
Kendra

extraordinary venture. He sought to combine his passion for the latest tenets of contemporary astronomy with the most ancient and sacred of his beliefs. The plan of the city is based on a nine-square mandala corresponding to the *navagraha* or nine planets. The void in the central square he used for the palace garden. (Because of the presence of a hill, a corner square was moved diagonally across.)[16]

For Correa this formal act provided an "origin" for his own aesthetic insight. Even though there is no hill in sight, Correa's design, through an aesthetic sleight-of-hand, remembers S. Jai Singh's formal act by dislocating one of the nine squares of the plan to make an opening that forms the entrance into the self-enclosed cosmos of the building (fig. 8).

There is neither any causal connection nor any deep "nonmanifest" principle linking Jain's interpretation of Jaipur's plan with Correa's plan for the Kendra. The latter is simply an aesthetic "manifest" displacement of the former. Correa's legerdemain produces an aesthetic event that represents another "original" aesthetic response. It is an aesthetic response to an aesthetic response, a representation of a representation. It matters little that Jain's analysis is not verifiable historically. Correa is responding to the cogency of Jain's representation that highlights S. Jai Singh's formal act. For Jain this facilitated a framework for architectural and urban analysis; for Correa it furnished an "original" through which he could construct a representation that was the genesis of his plan.

In this context it is instructive to examine the following passage by Correa that contains the most elaborate articulation of "aesthetic insight." It discloses and participates in a larger world view, which I will analyze as that of the postcolonial artist. It contains a host of negotiations that are transacted between ancient Hindu philosophy and its dominant "others"—Islam and Christianity. They are mediated by the legitimizing authority of Western science that is, paradoxically, used to legitimize the aesthetic agency of the artist who has already been identified as Eastern.

According to Hinduism, when the cycles of reincarnation are finally over, and the *atma* (the individual soul) is released from each of us, it goes to Brahman (to the center of [the] energy field). The analogy to the black

16. Correa, "Public, Private and Sacred," 96.

holes of contemporary physics is astounding. Energy devours itself and the individual soul... goes not to an eternal reward in Heaven or the Garden of Paradise [read the Western Judeo-Christian and Islamic tradition], but down the vortex at the center of a black hole. How incredible that such a concept should have surfaced so many thousands of years ago. As the noted French academician, Gaston Bachelard, has pointed out, the intuitive insight of the artist (or for that matter the seer) cannot be explained through the cause-and-effect structure of scientific reasoning but, like a depth charge, explodes in the center of our being, releasing to the surface the debris of our unconscious. This is why the invisible, the mythic, the sacred, will always be central to art—and our lives.[17]

In the microcosm of this passage Correa's circular world view is articulated around the "intuitive insight of the artist." He begins with a universal invocation of the nonmanifest, differentiates the particular, appeals through an "analogy" to the weight of scientific reason, and finally returns at a higher plane of enlightenment to the original centrality of the "invisible, the mythic, the sacred."

The all-encompassing cosmic order described by the mandalas is legitimized in Correa's essay by its verification by the neutral, cosmic (in the sense of universal) claims of science. In effect what is ultimately legitimized, in hindsight by science, is aesthetic insight that has already been identified as "Indian." Posited thus, as preceding and outside the cause-and-effect mechanism of reason, Indian aesthetic insight is that faculty that requires the scaffolding of Western science to reconstruct it, and then does away with it. Even though in abstraction aesthetic insight is claimed to precede and to have access to depths unavailable to science, the latter's retrospective validation of the former is the necessary, though denied, precondition that enables aesthetic insight's claim to autonomy.

Identity Production in the Postcolonial Frame

I am not arguing that Correa's essay simply masks claims to an "Indian" identity under the guise of aesthetic insight that is characterized as non-Western. Correa presents innumerable examples from the Western architectural canon to back up aesthetic insight's claims to universality. Rather, I am articulating the manner in which claims to

17. Correa, "Public, Private and Sacred," 92.

universality negotiate and are negotiated by the particular. For it is these negotiations that are the name of the game in the formation and articulation of the postcolonial identity, as they were of the colonial.

In the play of representation, the question or sense of origins or the original does not disappear. Correa described the "intuitive insight of the artist" to be "like a depth charge [that] explodes in the center of our being, releasing to the surface the debris of our unconscious." At one level one can interpret this as simply symptomatic of the superficial and ideologically suspect belief in the deep-rooted connection between the unconscious intuitions of the artist and the larger collective unconscious that is named the mandala, the nonmanifest, the essence, the sacred.

At another level, however, it can be interpreted as a metaphor for beginnings. A depth charge that explodes in the depths of one's unconscious is not a conception that locates beginning in an "originary idea"—in the sense of the pure ordering presence of a transcendental creative impulse. Rather it locates beginning in an "original" nonpresence, a disintegration, which can be detected only after the fact from the debris scattered on the surface of our manifest consciousness. After the fact there is only debris, and no amount of "plumbing the depths" and "searching for origins" can locate the site of the explosion. Correa's genesis of the plan of Jawahar Kala Kendra is simply an after-the-fact, aesthetic transformation of the debris, of which the original act is always already lost.

From such a perspective it is the Kendra plan's graphic character that sets up associations through a visual recognition with both the nine-square mandala and the old city of Jaipur. It functions as the active maker of contemporary identity—precisely by being "non-depth," non-insight. Correa's design does not dissolve the question of the Indian identity. It simply disorients it, uses it and casts it aside, inhabits it and critiques it. In other words, it parodies the impossible stereotype "Indian" by suspending it within distancing quotation marks.

To rephrase the above: For those of "us" caught in the double bind of asserting a different regional identity and simultaneously preventing its normative essentialization, the question one must ask is: If the "originary" meaning and idea of the aesthetic trace that one meets as debris is always already lost in an unknown and unknowable depth explosion, how is one to even anchor the debris in this unknown, unknowable

51

past event—let alone measure the strength and depth of this anchor in its claim to be an "authentic" or "true" representation of the catachresis "Indian"? I would suggest that this desire for anchoring is best left suspended. I would propose the somewhat duplicitous strategy of suspending a parodic veil that would reveal by concealing—that would re-cover—the unfathomable depths of the "truth" of our "identities." Such a veil can also, like a pliable and multicentered fishing net, better resist the penetrating desires of hegemonical cultural tendencies.

To pick the debris and knit it into the overlaid strains of the veil is not an easy task or a light matter. Each piece of debris is weighed down and pushed around by competing discursive formations. And the dominant carries the greatest weight and holds most pieces securely in place. One cannot simply dive in and transform the patterns willy-nilly. It is a question of power and strategy and of guarding against the tendency to be caught in one's own net.

This does not mean that Jawahar Kala Kendra is an exemplary postcolonial architectural object, or Charles Correa an exemplary architect. I do not think there are any exemplars; exemplification, even as one must necessarily use it, is precisely what one must guard against.

A House for Josephine Baker
Karen Burns

Spatial Secrets

The (question of the) representation of "race" in and around Adolf Loos's Josephine Baker House is now an open secret of contemporary architectural criticism— "open" because "race" (the term used by critics to name a host of issues) is tacitly acknowledged as one of the topics raised by looking at the house, "secret" because the opening provided by the incantation of the word "race" is quickly abandoned by criticism. Inevitably, the word recedes and the sentence moves forward, passing on to other subjects.

Beatriz Colomina's feminist reading of the Baker House in her important and groundbreaking essay, "The Split Wall: Domestic Voyeurism," has been castigated for its apparent failure to explicate the topic of race it overtly raises as an "issue."[1] According to the logic of the secret, Colomina's essay names the contents of the secret but fails to communicate them. However, in critics' haste to address feminism's failure of race memory, they have forgotten that feminism has made a *different* opening for architecture. Even as feminist theory's ability to think alterity otherwise has been under question, feminism has introduced the ideas "difference" and "identity" to architecture. Colomina noted that "The Josephine Baker house represents a shift in the sexual status of the body. This shift involves determinations of race and class more than gender."[2] In another recent essay, "Undressing Architecture: Fashion, Gender, and Modernity," Mary McLeod observes, "The zebra striping of the facade is as attention-getting as Baker's own dynamic and original presence. Most probably, this was not just an issue of 'negritude,' but one of sex."[3] These feminist critics were the first to articulate the need for a theorization of racial difference in relation to the Josephine Baker discourse. It is important that this difference in the discourse is noted, and that our indebtedness to this work is acknowledged.

As a number of feminists have observed, race cannot be merely added to the existing feminist recipe, correcting its erroneous exclusion. Attention to the other axes of difference within the term "woman" can result in difference merely being incorporated into a redrawn category of the same.[4]

1. This is the critique of Beatriz Colomina's essay "The Split Wall: Domestic Voyeurism," in Beatriz Colomina, ed., *Sexuality & Space* (New York: Princeton Architectural Press, 1992), 72–128. The critique was published in *Appendix: Theory Culture Praxis*, vol. 1, no. 1, (1993).
2. Colomina, "Split Wall," 98.
3. Mary McLeod, "Undressing Architecture: Fashion, Gender, and Modernity," in Deborah Fausch et. al., ed., *Architecture: in Fashion* (New York: Princeton Architectural Press, 1994), 67.
4. Some feminists have argued that the radical challenge to the category "woman" from those who are implicitly or explicitly excluded from it is not a demand for inclusion into an already preconceived paradigm but, as Annamarie Jagose puts it, "a far more unsettling question concerning the foundation and authority of the category itself." See Jagose, *Lesbian Utopics* (New York: Routledge, 1994), 15.

The open secret, D. A. Miller observes, is a secret intimated so as not to be told.[5] In theatrically keeping the secret it has already been given away. What is included in the secret is already known, but what is excluded—or rather covered over—is the mechanism of secrecy itself. Miller asks, what is it that covers secrecy, not what does secrecy cover?

This is not an essay about unmasking (uncovering) the contents of the secret but one of addressing questions to the terms delimiting inquiries into difference, identity, and architecture. For example, following Miller one might ask, What if the rhetorical act of deferral is not peculiar to feminist readings of the Josephine Baker House but to nearly all of the architectural essays, to the white architectural imaginary that contemplates that building? What if it is not so much a problem of exposing race as an issue, but the problem of criticism's effective modes of explanation—of a criticism whose mode is to endlessly defer that elaboration, even whilst inextricably enmeshed within it?

In taking deferral not as an error, a problem to be exposed, but as a mode of thinking about racial difference, I want to attend to the terms in which certain ideas of architecture *as* racial difference have been thought. The topic and the terms in which it is posed ("race and architecture") has a history, or histories. One of these histories is the discourse on the Josephine Baker House. And it is there, in that swirling movement of words, that I begin, not with the announcement of race and sex as a fact, but with a question, How does the secret of racial difference and alterity work for architecture?

To begin by asserting that "race" is not a fact that must be added to accounts of the Josephine Baker House (as another minutely specified difference to attain a totality) offers me a different starting point, for example, by asking instead, How does the discourse on that building bring racial difference as architecture into play?[6] It is not that race needs to be thought as an addition; it has already been wrought in particular ways. These matter. How have the terms "race" and "Baker" been mobilized? By whom? For whom? What tasks do they perform? What actions do they enable?[7] Addressing these questions is one way to begin thinking otherwise, as a way of changing (and not restating) the discussion's available terms and repertoire.

54   5. D. A. Miller, *The Novel and the Police* (Berkeley: University of California Press, 1988), 194. "For I have had to intimate my secret, if only not to tell it, and conversely, in theatrically continuing to keep my secret, I have already rather given it away."

6. Meaghan Morris, "The Man In The Mirror: David Harvey's Condition of Postmodernity," *Theory, Culture & Society* 9 (1992): 272, notes that a feminist critique that ignores issues of gender, race, and ethnicity "counterposes to its critique of 'exclusion' not a demand for inclusion—an adding of minutely specified differences ('etc.') to attain totality—but a politics of *conjunction* and *disjunction*."

7. I am paraphrasing some of the opening gambits of Meaghan Morris's essay "Metamorphoses at Sydney Tower," Australian *Cultural History* 10 (1991): 19.

Enclosure

Since the mid-sixties, Loos's commentary has appeared regularly in English, with essays and books now running at a steady flow. The Josephine Baker House appears as one episode in the larger story of Adolf Loos, modernist architect. Many of these writings have worked the genre of architectural biography (the man and his works), but when faced with the Baker House, it becomes apparent that authorial origin is not always a satisfactory mode of explanation.

Numerous commentaries about the Baker House intimate that there is something *else* beyond the immediate horizon of the description that is necessary to make sense of the building. In 1966, in the first major English translation of a monograph on Adolf Loos, Ludwig Münz and Gustav Künstler grappled with this sensation of "something else," observing, "Africa: that is the image conjured up more or less firmly by a contemplation of the model." In a small essay on Loos published in 1982, Joseph Rykwert also struggles to define that imprecise referent that will explain the building's elements, its roofs, volumes and windows. He settles on the comment that these forms are "all deliberately exotic, almost African." A recently translated Loos monograph also stumbles on those same windows, roof, etc. that stumped Rykwert, and its author Panayotis Tournikiotis's commentary on the house *as* enigma offers up the enigmatic as a judgment, "an exotic and mysterious image, vaguely evocative of African architecture."[8]

Each of these analyses is structured around a movement of citation and evasion. A particular referent—Africa—is evoked, then evaded. The secret of how to make sense of the house is given away; Africa is the key to unlocking the building's meaning, but Africa floats as an imprecise referent, its elaboration forever deferred. To invoke the logic of the secret, the contents are intimated but cannot be unraveled. The reading does not keep the secret in the dark (Africa is the key) but the possibilities for argument are clouded by the difficulties of apparently seeing that continent with clarity.

Keeping the sign "Africa" vague activates myths of Africa (mysterious, exotic, ungraspable), myths not in the sense of "false belief" but as effective modes of explanation and definition.[9] It is also part of what Gayatri Chakravorty Spivak has called the "conventionally sanctioned carelessness about identities."[10] Which bit of Africa, which community, which ethnicity, what historical moment surrounds this "Africa"? Keeping the.

8. Ludwig Münz and Gustav Künstler, *Adolf Loos*, trans. Harold Meek (London: Thames and Hudson, 1966), 195. Joseph Rykwert, *The Necessity of Artifice* (London: Academy Editions, 1982), 72. Panayotis Tournikiotis, *Adolf Loos*, trans. Marguerite McGoldrick (New York: Princeton Architectural Press, 1994), 95. Other Loos's works consulted include Heinrich Kulka, *Adolf Loos Das Werk des Architekten* (Vienna: Anton Schroll, 1931); Benedetto Gravagnuolo, *Adolf Loos*, trans. C. H. Evans (New York: Rizzoli, 1982); Burkhard Rukschio and Roland Schachel, *Adolf Loos* (Salzburg: Residenz Verlag, 1982); Pierre Mardaga, ed., *Adolf Loos 1870–1933* (Brussels: Galerie des Princes, 1985); Paul Groenendijk and Piet Vollaard, *Adolf Loos House for Josephine Baker* (Rotterdam: Uitgeverij, 1985); Colomina "The Split Wall," 73–130; McLeod, "Undressing Architecture," 38–123.

9. I am paraphrasing Meaghan Morris, "Aspects of Current French Feminist Literary Criticism,"

sign "Africa" at the level of vagueness reproduces colonialist operations of "othering" that depend on, and must work at, a certain level of generalization for their effects. This "other" is defined as finally unknowable, beyond the limits of precise definition, an empty space to be (covertly) filled.

Instead of describing this move in the familiar terms of identification and disavowal, the citation/evasion move may have another logic. I read it as a strategy that this architectural discourse has for solving the problems raised by the referent "Africa." Africa is not only the figurative outside (as bearer of racial difference) but also a figure for other discourses (their difference and identity) outside architecture's specified boundaries. Another discourse is gestured at, but its elaboration, its possibilities are located elsewhere, outside the confines of this one.

Thus, the Josephine Baker House commentaries are continually negotiating the problem, What counts as material to be included in the history of architecture? Some sense of how this became a problem at a particular historical moment can be sensed by comparing the writings from the mid-sixties to an earlier essay. The earliest description of the house (if an origin can ever be located) is Heinrich Kulka's sparse notes, published in what has been called "the first definitive volume"[11] to appear on the work of Loos. Published in Vienna in 1931 Kulka's text is brief:

> The different uses of the rooms explain the various heights, sizes, and positions of the windows. That the first floor of the facade at the corner is without windows is explained by the fact that a skylight had been proposed over the large swimming pool situated in the corner of that building. It had been intended to clad the facade with black and white marble slabs.[12]

Kulka's sober prose relies only on the citation of Baker's name and a tidy physical description. Perhaps it did not need to say much more. Four years prior to the 1931 publication Baker had visited Vienna, and her visit became the scene of a very public, racist, and political media storm.[13] The citation of Baker's name in an architectural description may have been all that was needed, given the cultural currency of "Josephine Baker" as a referent in 1930s public discourses about race, sexuality, and "moral purity." As the referent became less familiar, an uncommon part of circulating media discourse, perhaps there was an increasing necessity to explain and fix it.

56   *Hecate* 2 (1979): 64.

10. Gayatri Chakravorty Spivak, "Imperialism and Sexual Difference," *Oxford Literary Review* vol. 8 no. 1–2 (1986): 230.

11. Tournikiotis, *Adolf Loos*, 173.

12. Kulka, *Adolf Loos*, 41. The English translation has been kindly provided by Astrid, Horst, and Christine Huwald.

13. Phyllis Rose gives an account of this episode in her *Jazz Cleopatra: Josephine Baker In Her Time* (London: Vintage, 1991), 127–32. Other Baker biographies consulted in this text include the posthumously published autobiography by Josephine Baker and Jo Bouillon, *Josephine*, trans. Mariana Fitzpatrick (London: W. H. Allen, 1978); Alan Schroeder, *Josephine Baker* (New York: Chelsea House,

Architectural discourse on the Josephine Baker House seems continually disabled (and enabled) by the problem of constituting and regulating architecture's legitimate domains of reference. This discourse works hard to deny (while being drawn within) the intertextuality that is part of all text making.[14] It is, as Meaghan Morris observes, "the political issue of how and why we construct our contexts of reading and the practices that ensue."[15] The figure of Josephine Baker as the outside works doubly in architectural commentaries: as a figure of racial difference and as a figure of "issues" properly belonging elsewhere, in other discourses outside architecture's proper concerns.[16]

How does one explain the building once the familiar public discourses that materialize the building and that it materializes apparently disappear? As I read and reread the texts on the Baker House I wondered if their authors were trying to solve this problem not through the citation, as one might expect, of other historical discourses (newspaper commentaries, reviews, entertainment biographies) but through the phantasmatical recovery of Josephine Baker, her name, and, increasingly, her body.

Only two of the architectural essays I have read cite a biography of Baker as source material for their own readings.[17] In the attempt to recover Baker in order to read the house as a sign of its owner's attributes, the process of citation—the strategies of reference used to create a speaking position—are elided. Instead, architectural writers cite each others' texts, chasing each other around and around the enclosure.

Reading the Loos commentaries suggests another way of proceeding. I want to think about the problem of developing modes of reading as a problem of citation and reference and to examine how these modes are framed as three kinds of solutions to reading three different spaces. The Josephine Baker House narrative is structured into three scenes that simultaneously enable three scenarios of reading *as* three different spatial configurations: the "African" exterior, the unreadable relations of exterior/interior, and the most privileged space of all, the enclosed indoor swimming pool.

Exterior

Africa: that is the image conjured up more or less firmly by a contemplation of the model.　　　—Ludwig Münz and Gustav Künstler, 1966

1991); Bryan Hammond and Patrick O'Connor, *Josephine Baker* (Boston: Bulfinch Press, 1988); Jean-Claude Baker and Chris Chase, *Josephine: The Hungry Heart* (New York: Random House, 1993); and Stephen Papich, *Remembering Josephine* (Indianapolis, IN: Bobbs-Merrill, 1976). I have not been able to obtain Baker's autobiography as told to a biographer in Paris in 1927 when Baker was 21, that is, *before* Loos's design: Marcel Sauvage, *Les Mémoires de Josephine Baker* (Paris: RKA, 1927; reprinted in 1949). Two other unconsulted Baker biographies are Lynn Haney, *Naked at the Feast* (New York: Dodd, Mead, 1981) and Leo Guild, *Josephine Baker* (Los Angeles: Holloway House, 1976).
14. Meaghan Morris, *The Pirate's Fiancee: Feminism, Reading, Postmodernism* (London: Verso, 1988), 243.
15. Ibid., 6.
16. This is related to feminist concerns about the "function of images of 'Woman' to *signify* the

1
Josephine Baker
House, Adolf Loos,
Paris, 1927, model

What stands out most clearly is the Mediterranean appearance of the house.
—Benedetto Gravagnuolo, 1982

The sharp contrasted geometry of the volumes, the flat roofs, the large expanses of windowless wall are all deliberately exotic, almost African. As is the extraordinary facing of white and black alternating stripes of marble slabs.
—Joseph Rykwert, 1982

The appearance of the building recalls the architecture from southern countries and Africa: flat roofs, geometrical forms, small windows like holes in thick walls. The rest of the design intensifies the exotic character of the house.
—Paul Groenendijk and Piet Vollaard, 1985

The compactness of the volume, the flat roof, the small, low openings, the vast blind surfaces, and the bands of black and white marble created an exotic and mysterious image, vaguely evocative of African architecture.
—Panayotis Tournikiotis, 1994[18]

For many of the quotations cited above, a set of individual features (windows, flat roof, volumes) adds up to a recipe of African building. The quotes raise the possibility of reading histories of modernism differently, of not reading European modernism as a self-proclaimed project of disengaging with past categories of style and ornament, but as engaging in the figuration of a European colonial present.

For me, what is more interesting than assuming a relationship between modernism and colonialism is questioning how such assumptions are made. The Josephine Baker House discourse produces very precise effects though the authors' strategies of reference may be evasive. As I have noted, one of these effects is a certain reproduction of colonialist practices of generalized alterity. How does one avoid merely repeating this practice by unmasking its operations?

I would like to address these questions by discussing the facade's alternating marble bands that so bewitch criticism (fig. 1). These bands hover between literalism and abstraction. One of the most effective functions of built space is to work as metonym. Of

problem of (power) knowledge." See Meaghan Morris, "Things To Do With Shopping Centres," in Susan Sheridan, ed., *Grafts: Feminist Cultural Criticism* (London: Verso, 1988), 202.
17. McLeod, "Undressing Architecture," 114, footnote 103 cites Baker's 1949 (auto)biography. Groenendijk and Vollaard, *Adolf Loos House*, 36 cites Baker's 1976 biography in their list of references.
18. Münz and Künstler, *Adolf Loos*, 195; Gravagnuolo, *Adolf Loos*, 191; Rykwert, *Necessity of Artifice*, 72; Groenendijk and Vollaard, *Adolf Loos House*, 36; Tournikiotis, *Adolf Loos*, 95.

course either of these two positions in a binary of literalism/abstraction depends on the discourse from which one is reading. One person's literalism is another's abstraction. This is part of the bands' successful metonymic slide from both representing Baker *and* representing other culturally mythical discourses about the representation of the West and its other, and the representation of a white architectural imaginary.

Can the symbolic power of these bands, which resonate for Loos and other readers of the building, be explained in terms of Loos's fortunate aesthetic choice? The metonymic success of the bands, as literal referents and aesthetic abstraction, assumes a different hue when considered in relation to other discourses nominally outside architecture in Josephine Baker's particular costuming practices.

Costumes were crucial in the fabrication of Josephine Baker's corporeality in Europe in the late 1920s. In September 1925 Baker and her stage partner, Joe Alex, performed the *Danse Sauvage* as part of the Revue Négre at the Parisian Champs-Élysées Théâtre. This performance gave the nineteen-year-old Baker instant fame. She and Alex danced near naked with bands of feathers clustered around their waists, wrists, and ankles as they enacted a Parisian director's notion of the African, the exotic, the mysterious, and the "savage."[19]

The other costume with which Baker was so long identified, launched the following year in 1926 at the Folies-Bergère, was a skirt of fake bananas. Baker performed as Fatou, a native girl up a tree who is dreamt up by a white explorer sleeping under a mosquito net.[20] "Up" is the appropriate signifier. The banana costume was modified over the ensuing years until it became an absurdly obvious cluster of extended, pointy (even erect) phalluses. Banana skirts enacted, most dramatically, the role of Baker as a woman who does not have, but is the (increasingly, self-reflexive) home of, the phallus. Baker's costume quite literally inscribed her as the site for white European heterosexual desires and fantasies of potency. Sex and corporeality are conflated. This body comes to stand as sex, as the displaced desire of white men for black women, and a particular black woman stands for sex that cannot be thought as an attribute of white women.

Both the Fatou and *Danse Sauvage* costumes attached long, pointy, vertical stripes to a waistband. A band is something distinguished by color or aspect from the surface it crosses. It encircles and defines; it can be a trap, literally that with which a

19. Rose, *Jazz Cleopatra*, 81.
20. Ibid., 23.

person or thing is bound. (Certainly these banded costumes were something from which Baker had to escape in later years as she gained more control over her work, presenting herself through a much more glamorous and sophisticated stage persona.) These mid-1920s costumes used colored bands of feathers (the *Danse Sauvage*) or golden bananas (Fatou) to form vertical banding and striation over the body. Colored feathers or yellow bands alternated with stripes of flesh as the body appeared beneath the costume in rhythmic striations. In the mid-1930s Baker wore a spikier, bikini version of the earlier banana skirt. This costume might be read as Baker's revenge against the banana skirt's skin-flick enactment of difference. Bent phalluses swaying on a band became a prickly suit of armor.

These Fatou-ous signifiers, the feathers and bananas were continually reinscribed (and circulated) cultural icons in popular postcards and drawings of Baker's costumed body. In 1929 on a ship returning from South America, the architect Le Corbusier attended the ship's ball in drag. He cross-dressed as Josephine Baker by blackening his body and wearing a waistband of feathers.[21] This one, potent, item of clothing effectively cited the earliest Parisian stage costumes of Josephine Baker.

Is it mere serendipity that the Baker House facade uses banding as a form of ornamentation? Perhaps not. The banding successfully cites the costumes of the intended occupier and certain Africanist myths. At its most stark and crude the black and white banding remembers what some critics have termed the "epidermal schema."[22] In this formation, one of the body's organs, the skin, is located as the most visible sign of difference. Gayatri Spivak has argued that "color" is a derisive name for ethnicity, one that renders absurd the complexity of differences by stitching them back into the body's singular location.[23]

The bands of the building make—inform—the spectacle of difference for architectural critics. This spectacle can only be named by them as the sign "Africa," the sign of difference. Yet the critics seem strangely color blind. Numerous architectural writers have seen the house as a sign of difference and been blind to its representation of whiteness, its representation of themselves.

The black and white bands of the house appear physically equivalent; they occupy the same space. However, a fundamental asymmetry governs and orders the

21. See ibid., 152–153 and Baker and Bouillon, *Josephine*, 80–81.
22. Homi K. Bhabha takes up Franz Fanon's observations on the epidermal schema in his essay "The Other Question: Stereotype, Discrimination and the Discourse of Colonialism," in Homi K. Bhabha, *The Location of Culture* (London: Routledge, 1994), 78. For a feminist reading of Fanon's formulation in relation to questions of visibility and the cinema, see Mary Ann Doane, "Dark Continents: Epistemologies of Racial and Sexual Difference in Psychoanalysis and the Cinema," in her book *Femmes Fatales: Feminism, Film Theory, Psychoanalysis* (New York: Routledge, 1991), 209–48.
23. Spivak, "Imperialism and Sexual Difference," 235. This observation is pointedly retold in Baker's own on-stage identity. An expatriate African-American woman, making a career in Paris, is frequently asked to pass as an African. The over-visibility of the epidermal schema functions doubly for Baker, to

epidermal schema's hierarchy. Black is the visible color, the sign *of* color, while white functions as the unmarked term, the universal that values and marks other colors.

Curiously, the bands encasing the house signify the ambiguity of the border in its demarcation of racial difference.[24] Between the bands, between the slabs that bandage/suture together the categories "black" and "white" lies the border; this joint is the dividing line between the two categories. The joint is the legislative line, insisting on demarcation and separation of the categories. Yet equally it is an interface conjoining the categories it distinguishes. As Annamarie Jagose observes, "The slash of the border is the very site at which the taxonomic closure it effects is also indefinitely deferred."[25] But can this double reading of the border's legislative force and its failure to achieve the taxonomic closure it desires be applied to the Baker House?

Whiteness operates in two locations in the Josephine Baker House. First, it registers among the banding. Although I have suggested whiteness dissimulates its status as a color, it can be argued that due to its position—between black bands, between the borders—that here, at least, it does not lie about its status as a color. Apparently, it comes clean, giving itself a visible presence in the epidermal schema black/white.

Second, whiteness registers its status as the determining color and disavows its value by slipping discretely into the background. The base of the building is white. White is not a color that proclaims, but a foundation. Whiteness dissimulates, passes *as* invisibility.[26]

In this way, the possible ambiguities of the border, their potential to be read as the infinite failure to specify the differences they legislate, does not finally happen at the Josephine Baker House. The drama of dissimulation and the power of the metonymic slide from facade to costumed skin is, I think, more forceful and overwhelming than the potentially critically optimistic registration of difference as deferral, of the way in which white (as one color) is only a deferral of black (another color). Both categories are color coded. Whiteness cannot pass as the unmarked term, off-loading the burden of "race" onto blackness.

The methods of citation, evasion, and studied vagueness that characterize the descriptions of the Baker House exterior offer some answers to the question of what the house stands for in architectural criticism: racial difference *and* the difference of other discourses. The reading of the border suggests that architecture might function metonymically, but the commentaries bordering on that possibility must stop that slide as it

reduce her to pure biology and to efface the displacements that fashion her own identity.

24. My reading of the irresolution of the border is indebted to Annamarie Jagose's essay "Slash and Suture," a chapter of her book, *Lesbian Utopics*, 136–57.

25. Ibid., 137.

26. Doane, "Dark Continents," 244.

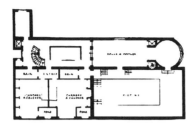 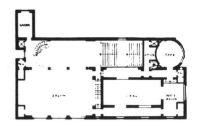

2
Josephine Baker
House, plans

opens up the possibility of something beyond the border of architecture. Studied vagueness might work as a strategy of containment and isolation. But when evasive (borderline) reading fails there is always recourse in the figure of the unreadable.

The Unreadable Interior

The interior cannot be guessed at by looking at the outside.
—Ludwig Münz and Gustav Künstler, 1966

In line with Loos's way of thinking, the exterior says nothing about the interior.
—Benedetto Gravagnuolo, 1982

In this project for a house for Josephine Baker Loos uses a number of elements we find in his other work: the closed character of the facades.
— Paul Groenendijk and Piet Vollaard, 1985

The compactness of the volume, the flat roof, the small, low openings, the vast blind surfaces and the bands of black and white marble created an exotic and mysterious image, vaguely evocative of African architecture, while providing no clues as to the interior. —Panayotis Tournikiotis, 1994[27]

If, as Beatriz Colomina has argued, writers have persisted in reading the architecture of the Baker House as attributes of Josephine Baker,[28] how might one understand these same writers' insistence that from the exterior the building's interior (fig. 2) is unreadable, unpenetrable by criticism?

Yet such a reading has been made. On the one hand the building's exterior veils the vision of the critic by sending the referent "Africa" into a hazy and apparently unfocusable, imprecise reading (a smudge), and, on the other, the exterior presents a blankness, rather than a transparent path for criticism's line of sight. Vision fails criticism as insight.

Vision is often associated with mastery and assumed (but ultimately failed) distance.[29] However, these readings of the Baker House suggest a form of critical insight based on a protected and limited way of seeing. The Baker House seems to be a project that confronts (or is read as confronting) critics, again and again, with their own fallibility.

62   27. Münz and Künstler, *Adolf Loos*, 195; Gravagnuolo, *Adolf Loos*, 191; Groenendijk and Vollaard, *Adolf Loos House*, 34; Tournikiotis, *Adolf Loos*, 95.
28. Colomina, "Split Wall," 97.
29. See for example Griselda Pollock's "Modernity and the Spaces of Femininity," which is prefaced by a quote from Luce Irigaray, "More than other senses, the eye objectifies and masters." The essay is reprinted in Norma Broude and Mary D. Garrard, ed., *The Expanding Discourse: Feminism and Art History* (New York: Harper Collins, 1992), 245.

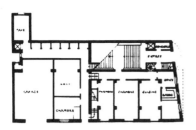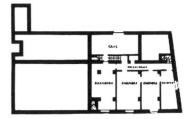

It eludes the project of "interpretation" that nominally guides architectural criticism. Current modish strategies of reading might write the house as a triumphant excess that can never be recuperated by criticism, or as the moment when architectural theory and history touch the limits of their own knowledge.

However, as Loos's biographers always strive to remind the reader, the failure of a facade's transparency is ultimately decipherable as authorial origin: the author decided to reverse the tried-and-true terms of criticism (exterior must reveal interior) and build a blank or blind wall. Criticism itself opens again, and closes, the problem of reference.

Perhaps the puzzle of the Baker House can be solved by looking elsewhere, to another discourse, to the biography of Josephine Baker. Since architectural writing continually attributed features taken to belong to Josephine Baker as features of the house, were critics narrating a story about Baker's own interior?

Is it that Baker's house and body possess an unreadable interior, or is it that they provide a different model of the body, one that can be described as all surface, one that radically confounds the surface/depth binary.[30] Or does a conventional binary model operate in this text, against which Baker's house and body can be construed as lacking?

The figuration of the body as an inner/outer binary has featured in the recent reconceptualization of subjectivity. In Michel Foucault's analysis, the binary erases the social work of inscription. The interior is a privileged trope for the soul. Occupying the body's internal cavities, the soul is the interior space intrinsic to the substance of a particular body, the locale of that body's sovereign will.[31] Foucault's reading of the inscription of an internal space *on the body* displaces the spatial relations assumed by the inner/outer binary. Rewriting Foucault's theorization of the soul as something produced by social inscription *on* the body, Judith Butler observes that acts, gestures, and desire produce the semblance of an internal core or substance on the surface of the body.[32]

Neither Foucault nor Butler in the texts I am citing address the question of corporeal inscription as cultural difference, ethnicity, and race.[33] However, Foucault and Butler's location of the body's surface as the site for social inscription might assist in negotiating Spivak's criticism of the epidermal schema. Spivak argues against the ridiculously simple and singular nature of the epidermal schema's insistence on skin as *the* visible

30. Theorists of the corporeal such as Vicky Kirby have argued (quoting Foucault's tracing of the workings of history as it is inscribed in the "nervous system, in temperament, in the digestive apparatus"), "The body's surfaces continue into the 'interior.' Paradoxically the surface is both the thing which supposedly divides and secures inside and outside and the thing that holds them together. Foucault's notion of inscription, which implies a surface to be written on, is an extraordinary surface that includes the bodies' depths and questions the division between interior and exterior." Kirby, "Corporeal Habits: Addressing Essentialism Differently," *Hypatia* vol. 6 no. 3 (Fall 1991): 21, note 20.
31. Michel Foucault, *Discipline and Punish: The Birth of the Prison*, trans. Alan Sheridan (Harmondsworth, UK: Penguin, 1982), 29–30.
32. Judith Butler, "Gender Trouble, Feminist Theory, and Psychoanalytic Discourse," in Linda J.

sign of difference. Locating all social inscription as a marking of surface, in the full complexity of that term (where does the body's surface begin and end?) places the skin, one organ, within a multiple network of corporeal organs, cells, and tissues. Reading, which is one form of social inscription, brings various parts of the corporeal to the surface. There is no natural, essential connection between skin and racial difference. But the intensity of focus on the epidermal schema conveniently ignores all the other work carried out by inscription on bodies.

Theorizing the importance of the fantasy of the internal, Butler explores the interior figure in psychoanalytic descriptions of the acquisition of a subject's identity. The structuring binary of surface/interior and its position in the description of psychic identity have a home, too, in architecture. While film and literary genres have rendered the domestic interior as an allegory of the psychic lives of its inhabitants, the architectural interior may be projected as a topography of the individual's own interior life. The inhabitants' sexual and psychic identities are worked by and within the spatial settings of the interior and its ritualized, sexual dramas.

Given these conventions, what are we to make of a house, interior, and inhabitant who are all surface? I do not believe that architectural commentaries rewrite the received terms of inner/outer body and subject as Judith Butler does. If the most commonplace meanings of these corporeal descriptions haunt the Baker House descriptions within this metaphysical binary, Baker cannot be the divided subject who is the subject of psychoanalytic inquiry. Without an interior, she has no possibility for an internal psychic space and no fantasized locale for the identity of self. This lack of interiority, or deferral, renders her not only as different from other inhabitants, but as someone whose interior is completely unknowable.

Ironically the Josephine Baker House was never built. All that remains is a model and plans whose interiors we are unable to inhabit. Within architecture, then, Baker's interiority is in one sense never realized; it is eternally deferred.[34]

These theoretical moves of forever pointing out exclusion and failure often leads to a dead end. It assumes a particular reading of the subject as a problem for criticism (and, similarly, for feminism). In the end it does not explain how the logic of criticism works in the Baker House commentaries: what tasks it performs, what actions it

64   Nicholson, ed., *Feminism/Postmodernism* (New York: Routledge, 1990), 136.

33. Judith Butler has written several essays addressing questions of ethnicized, raced corporeality in her book *Bodies That Matter* (New York: Routledge, 1993).

34. This reading was suggested by Rose Lucas at a presentation of an earlier incarnation of this paper to a Women's Studies symposium at Monash University in November 1993.

enables. To keep retrieving Baker as an exemplum of alterity is to keep pinning her back against the wall, to that place already assigned to her by criticism.

Thinking again of the unreadable interior, perhaps it has another function, apart from the invocation of certain myths of unreadable Africa in the logic of criticism. To produce the interior as a secretive place, one whose secrets cannot be *guessed*, at this stage of the story, creates narrative suspense. This is a function of critical writing. It sets the stage for the final drama of the interior. If the critic's dream of unimpeded visibility is blocked by the apparently mute surfaces of this place, it is recovered in the readings of the internal swimming pool, a place where criticism finds and flexes its own identity.

The Pool

On the first floor, low passages surround the pool. They are lit by wide windows visible on the outside, and, from them, thick, transparent windows are let into the side of the pool, so that it was possible to watch swimming and diving in its crystal-clear water, flooded with light from above: an underwater revue, so to speak.—Kurt Unger, "one of Loos's closest collaborators," from a 1935 letter, quoted by Ludwig Münz and Gustav Künstler, 1966

The passage and the boudoir, moreover, have safety glass windows into the pool through which you might see the people bathing in the water. A naughty extravaganza you might say. Of course. —Joseph Rykwert, 1982

The water flooded with light, the refreshing swim, the voyeuristic pleasure of underwater exploration—these are the carefully balanced ingredients of this gay architecture. —Benedetto Gravagnuolo, 1982

The walls of the swimming pool have thick glass windows in order to watch the hostess swim and dive, from the corridors; with the light from above, a veritable "underwater revue." —Paul Groenendijk and Piet Vollaard, 1985

Oblong windows in the walls of its swimming pool allowed a glimpse of the swimmer's underwater ballet. This rediscovery of the feminine body and a voyeur's pleasure were indicative of Loos's eroticism, expressed in a poetic game of desire and confession. . . . Four long windows in the corridors and in the small salon allowed observation of the swimmers.

—Panayotis Tournikiotis, 1994[35]

Adolf Loos's design for the Josephine Baker House was never built. A photograph of the model and drawings are the only material that architectural criticism has to imagine what this house might have been. Photographs of the exterior walls and roof have been published again and again, but the infinite spaces of the home's interior, infinite because never built in model or full-scale form, are inhabited by an architectural imaginary that finally allows itself not to metonymically imagine, but to *see* Josephine Baker.

The swimming pool is the most described internal space of the house. No doubt this is partly due to the pool's novelty within the familial domestic genre of bedrooms, bathrooms, and kitchen. However it is not the phenomenal experience of swimming in a strangely enclosed space that fascinates writers, but the liminal interior of walls and windows, the vista of the pool when seen through a window.

Sometime in the mid-eighties, a small difference in the weave transformed the pattern of the Baker House descriptions. The pool, which from the 1930s to the 1980s had been peopled with a mass of swimmers, cleared, its waters subsided and only one swimmer was left, Josephine Baker.[36] The writer watches the swimmer. "The swimmer," "the hostess," "the feminine body" are the words critics use. Josephine Baker is not referred to by name, but Baker's ghost hovers in the swimmer. Perhaps names would eloquently point to the intimacy that is not there but imagined by one body observing another.

The figure of a figure looking through a narrow slot may just be a *mise en abime* of the critic's own activity. This is the moment when a text projects the conditions of its own readability through a figure, image, or representation of the story-telling relationship. This *mise en abime* is defined by two poles: window and water. They represent transparency, of reading as unimpeded visibility, a criticism without opaque remnants (referents). The critic gazing onto a view through the window imagines an unimpeded visibility, the deciphering of spaces, an architecture without secrets. However, the window is not only a medium for seeing through, but a screen to reflect the critic's and the discourse's desires. Transparency, framed as the power of the critic's vision, is one reason why the discussion of

35. Münz and Künstler, *Adolf Loos*, 195; Gravagnuolo, *Adolf Loos*, 192; Groenendijk and Vollaard, *Adolf Loos House*, 34; Tournikiotis, *Adolf Loos*, 18, 98.

36. Tournikiotis's text is ambiguous on this point; he moves between an image of a singular female swimmer and a group of swimmers. Thanks to Clare Jacobson for pointing out this anomaly.

the Baker House cannot be a project of ripping off the mask of criticism and exposing its racism. Critical revelation as exposure reproduces knowledge within the existing terms of discussion. These crucial relations of difference are not behind or underneath but essential to an act of reading that construes disinterested knowledge as the product of criticism's gaze.

Water as a transparent medium exposes Baker to views, as the "feminine body," pure corporeality, pure sexuality. But is water a fluid material, something merely to see through and thus neutral, or is it frozen? For window and pool are not transparently equivalent terms. Criticism freezes Baker in the pool. She is rarely sighted in any other domestic space. Water as a sign of nature offers her a place without history, without time. "But he did not look down on her, she represented to him Holy, untainted Nature," reported a contemporary of Adolf Loos on his description of Baker.[37] It freezes, effaces, the active process of myth formation that insists on her as an embodiment of nature.

But there is a crack in the relentless glaciers of criticism. Writers are also frozen into position on one side of the window. The figure of the window frame may not offer up a vision of criticism's insight, as much as a fear of proximity. The scene at the pool is the only moment for the possible conjunction between writing and subject, a moment of temporality. The frame offers the safety of physical, spatial separation.

Since looking does not automatically ensure distance from the subject (although this is a favored trope of some current modes of feminist thought)[38] the figure of the window could also indicate the fear of touching, of criticism's proximity (investment in) its own subject and the fear of touching the "issue" of race. In the end, the window touches the critic's body and protects his flesh, deferring an encounter with the imagined other.

The process of "othering" is a two-way activity. The icy hold of iteration on all the descriptions of the Baker House effaces the differences among individual authors, who consolidate themselves as a universal, white, Western self. It is, however, a small price to pay for the power to speak and to set the conditions of enunciation.

To imagine other terms—terms beyond the limits of reading Baker's "place" as a place in the pool and as the object of a one-way critic's gaze, with Baker's line of sight blocked by her own watery window reflection, gazed at without being able to gaze out ("the voyeur's pleasure" of one description); terms that acknowledge the critic's own complicity—is also to imagine a way of looking and speaking back.

37. Karin Michaelis, quoted in Rukschio and Schachel, *Adolf Loos*, 324. Translation courtesy of Astrid, Christine, and Horst Huwald.
38. See note 28.

3
Adolf and Elsie Loos,
August 1921

4
Josephine Baker,
Berlin, 1928

Asking questions about the construction of Josephine Baker's subjectivity could involve studying other discursive practices, other than the discourse of architecture. Josephine Baker's biography is one place to start—the discursive codes with which, and within which, she operates. I have in mind the kinds of distinctions Judith Butler makes between two views, the first that

> agency is an attribute of persons, presupposed as prior to language and power, inferred from the structure of the self; in the second, agency is the effect of discursive conditions which do not for that reason control its use; it is not a transcendental category, but a contingent and fragile possibility opened up in the midst of constituting relations.[39]

This is why my recourse to biography as a set of worked discursive codes is different from explanations that take authorial origin as the goal of criticism (as the cause of actions). There is, to begin, Baker's practice of reversing the terms of the discussion. Adolf Loos recalls that after first meeting and dancing with her in a Viennese club, Baker gave him a "big coin," complimenting him on his performance as a professional (*Eintänzer*), an idiomatic expression that also means "professional gigolo."[40] In this account it is Loos whose body bears (wears) the force of sexuality, money, and performance. Perhaps, after flipping through the published photographs of the huge Loos Albertina archive, it might be Loos rather than Josephine Baker who would occupy that pool. Several photos reveal Loos, standing proud on the beach in his bathers, a moment of studied corporeal display (fig. 3).

Baker's own off-stage descriptions suggest she might have been more comfortable making a grand entrance on the stair or watching from the salon rather than cavorting in the pool (fig. 4). Baker wrote of this period in her posthumously published autobiography:

> The white imagination sure is something when it comes to blacks.... Articles in which I barely recognized myself continued to fill the press.... I read such statements with the same astonishment I imagine a child would feel when a ball he has thrown crashes through a window.... Since I personified the savage on the stage, I tried to be as civilized as possible in daily life.[41]

39. Judith Butler, "For a Careful Reading," in *Feminist Contentions: A Philosophical Exchange: Seyla Benhabib, Judith Butler, Drucilla Cornell, Nancy Fraser* (New York: Routledge, 1995), 137.
40. Rukschio and Schachel, *Adolf Loos*, 323. For the translation and careful explanation of the word's double-entendre I thank Astrid, Christine, and Horst Huwald.
41. Baker and Bouillon, *Josephine*, 54–55.

Of a particular dress, she observed, "The finished dress was pink and the model became known as the *robe Joséphine*. I was learning the importance of names—having them, making them."[42] Her strategies of reference may have been the body, but the body has other significations apart from athletic beach games or nudity.

Her working of the vestimentary codes, her fabrication, brings the terms "savage" and "civilized" into contradictory proximity. She took the dress designer's signature as a statement of modernity (the latest word in style, a moment of complete contemporaneity) and affixed it to her own body. Eventually the dress became hers (the "*robe Joséphine*"), stamped with her own name. Of course one way to read this transformation is as another fable of colonialism (the efficacy of the modernizing power of dress), but this still asks people to ponder the tenuous nature of mask and robe swapping, of the politics of identity formation. The caption to one photograph in her autobiography reads, "A Study in Contrasts."[43]

The question of racial difference represented as Josephine Baker is not a simple one to be banished by the assertion of the importance of race in relation to Baker's representation. Her identities—an expatriate African-American who chooses, partly, to live away from the pincer of racist segregation in North American life, who is then asked in Paris to pass as an African and is later made a sub-lieutenant of the Women's Auxiliary of the Free French Air Force—are made out of disjunction and displacement, not as a totality of race, sex, and class.

Recently, a new theory about the Baker House has gripped architectural commentary. Despite the lack of archival evidence, this position asserts that the house was unsolicited.[44] One lecturer declared the project to be a homage from Loos to Baker.[45] When unsolicited attention can be read now as sexual harassment, these kinds of theoretical scenarios deserve some careful thought.

It matters, given there is no evidence either way as to who commissioned the project,[46] how we read Baker's refusal of Loos's house. I take it that Baker was carefully engaged in the "production of a speaking position as a matter of strategies of reference,"[47] and that the refusal of one kind of house for another mattered to her. Baker eventually bought a large mansion in the Parisian suburbs. In 1929 or 1930 she began living with her partner and manager, Pepito Abatino, at a house in the building she owned on the Avenue

42. Ibid., 55–56.
43. Ibid., unpaginated between pages 146 and 147.
44. Tournikiotis, *Adolf Loos*, 95.
45. David Dunster, public lecture "Josephine Baker and Modern Architecture," Melbourne University, 6 October 1993. Dunster observed that he did not know if it was a commission or a homage. I find it interesting that the possibility of it not being commissioned has arisen at this point in time.
46. Loos mentions a conversation with Josephine Baker where she laments the possibility of finding a suitable architectural plan. Rukschio and Schachel (*Adolf Loos*, 323) and Kulka (*Adolf Loos*, 41) point out that the project was intended for an actual site in Paris owned by Baker.
47. Morris, *Pirate's Fiancée*, 7.

Bugeaud, the probable site for Loos's design. Shortly thereafter Baker and Abatino together bought a house variously described as a "mansion" or "villa," Le Beau Chêne in the Parisian suburb of Le Vésinet. Some years later, in the late 1930s or in 1940 as she fled the advancing German army, Baker discovered and rented the chateau she called Les Milandes. She purchased the chateau in the late 1940s, at about the same time that she married Jo Bouillon.[48] "Mansion" and "history" are features that dramatically narrate the story of Baker's rapid class mobility. Why should not the emblems of aristocracy, of privilege as a birthright established by blood, be mobilized by a woman to rework narratives of class origin as fixed, and of racial difference as a fact of birth and blood, to acquire the difference and distinction of status and privilege? Baker's habits of dressing and cross-naming strategically realign her given references. Blood, birth, heritage, and inheritance may be read as similarly realigned in the story of her purchased property.

To interrupt the iterations of the story by citing Baker's autobiography is also a way of answering back, thinking otherwise about the function of Baker's apparition in the interior as spectacle. Rather than imagine what she might be, we might ask instead, What was her own retrospective reading of what she had done?

In and around the swimming pool, criticism is finally able to achieve its nominal project: to decipher spaces, to have spaces without secrets, to illuminate, to achieve unimpeded visibility. But all of these depend on summoning Baker's apparition. In the end, it is not so much a failure of criticism's vision (its lack of insight) but a problem of proximity and touch, of touching the issue of racial difference, the imagined figure of the other, and other discourses and materials. Like Baker's own practices, perhaps, it is not a project of specular mirroring but one of camouflage.

Reading Space

Meaghan Morris, an Australian writer, once observed of her own practices: In each case, I have tried not simply to find a way to "answer back," but to read these texts in question sympathetically in order to understand them *as* criticisms of those answers that my feminism might automatically provide, and so to use them to question my own assumptions and practices in the process of reading theirs.[49]

48. The Baker biographies provide conflicting dates for these purchases. Rose claims that the "chateau-like" Beau Chêne was purchased in 1929 and the "chateau" Les Milandes bought in 1936 (*Jazz Cleopatra*, 152, 185). Jean-Claude Baker, however, does not date the purchase of Le Beau Chêne ("her villa") but he describes Baker's move to this house at the beginning of a chapter set in late 1929/early 1930. He interviewed the family who lived at Les Milandes and dated Baker's *first* sighting of the chateau to 7 June 1940 (*Josephine*, 228). Stephen Papich recounts a tale told by Baker in which she and her partner Pepito Abatino discovered and rented the chateau in the early 1930s (*Remembering Josephine*, 141). Both Papich and Jean-Claude Baker at least agree that the chateau was not purchased until after the war. The Baker and Bouillon autobiography sets the purchase of Le Beau Chêne in a chapter describing Baker's life at the end of 1929 or beginning of

With Morris's wise words echoing in my head I have tried to read the Baker House commentaries other than as oppositional texts to be vanquished in the struggle to determine a correct reading. These discourses can be understood instead as explanations that use certain narrative and rhetorical strategies to solve fears, difficulties, and problems in criticism (how not to speak of certain issues while talking of them), thus in turn creating new dilemmas.

Morris's text suggests another valuable effect of reading other texts sympathetically so as not to merely return the existing terms of criticism. Her strategy provides a space in which one can think again about one's own presuppositions. In turn I have become wary of a critical strategy that merely points to racism without changing the available terms of discussion. Many of the architectural narratives I have discussed depend critically on the strategy of exposure, in particular Baker's own exposure to a critic's look, observed while unobservant of another's gaze. For this reason alone the dream of criticism cannot merely be one of making everything transparent to criticism, of just exposing racism. (This is not to say that racism should not be noted.) The question of representation is central to debates about who represents whom, what stories are told by whom and how, and what investments are made in taking such speaking positions. At the very least these issues cannot be resolved only on the question of the writer's apparent identity, since acknowledgment must be made of the institutional conditions of reading and writing, to the work of language itself.[50]

This project has been not the conventional one of reading architecture but of finding sources outside the architectural enclosure and learning from them. As a white Australian academic I learned much from reading Josephine Baker's autobiography, particularly from the telling of the conflict between how others chose to represent her and how she represented herself. Interrupting architecture's narrative with Josephine Baker's assessment of the other's representation of herself unsettles some presuppositions, even in the name of a sympathetic feminism, that Baker can be represented as a passive victim of architectural machinations. As importantly, her performance work suggests another way in which to read the facades of Loos's building in relation to Baker's own costuming practices on and off the stage. Out of the conditions in which she found herself she was able to fabricate her own body.

1930 (*Josephine*, 82). According to this account, Baker rented Les Milandes in 1937, the year she married Jean Lion (*Josephine*, 111–12) and decided to purchase it in 1947, but the authors do not give a date for her acquisition of the building (*Josephine*, 151). The very least that can be established is Baker's decision to purchase a suburban mansion/villa within one to two years after Loos's design.
49. Morris, *Pirate's Fiancée*, 6.
50. Gayatri Spivak, "Questions of Multiculturalism," in Sarah Harasym, ed., *The Post-Colonial Critic* (New York: Routledge, 1990), 63.

The Josephine Baker stories that have been told in architecture are significant. They cannot be merely revised, thrown out, or added onto. They tell us about things at the heart of architecture. There are different ways of telling and using stories but these architectural stories have been largely asymmetrical. They are dependent on silence and the evasion of issues of ethnicity and racial identity, and on the silence of Baker herself, as a subject to be looked at, rather than read and listened to. This essay suggests that secrecy and silence, quiet or anxious stillness, and evasiveness make certain kinds of stories.

Thanks to Gülsüm Baydar Nalbantoğlu and Wong Chong Thai for several years of hard work and vision, from the initial conference in Singapore to the fruition of the project as this publication. Thanks to RMIT University for a travel grant to cover my expenses to Singapore. The Center for Women's Studies at Monash University provided an opportunity to publicly present an earlier version of this paper and the audience returned a generous reading. Astrid, Horst, and Christine Huwald graciously translated Loos's material from the German originals. Thanks to John Biln, Mirjana Lozanovska, Stephen Cairns, and Helene Furjan.

Re-Surfacing:
Architecture, *Wayang*, and the "Javanese House"
Stephen Cairns

Introduction
I would like to begin by citing two excerpts from journal entries that record the experiences of two European travelers in different parts of Asia at different times.

Constantinople, Ottoman Empire, 13 December 1856
Started alone for Constantinople and, after a terrible long walk, found myself back where I started. . . . Just like getting lost in a wood. No plan to streets. Pocket compass. Perfect labyrinth. Narrow. Close, shut in. If one could but get up aloft, it would be easy to see one's way out. If you could but get up into tree. Soar out of the maze. But no. No names to the streets no more than to natural allies among the groves. No numbers. No anything.

Yogyakarta, Indonesia, 11 February 1991
I biked down the Malioboro this morning, had a name card made, posted some letters, and eventually got to the *Kraton*. This time the front section— *Pagelaran* and *Siti Hinggil*—was open. I saw a good detailed model of the whole *Kraton* complex, including the Sultan's quarters. I took quite a few exciting shots of the model, despite the scratched Perspex cover. Internally the daughters' quarters etc. are orientated north-south.

The first excerpt is from Herman Melville's account of his visit to the Middle East in 1856,[1] while the second is from the journal I kept during a period of architectural fieldwork in Indonesia in 1991. In comparing the two accounts, it struck me that Melville's frustration at not being able to get "up aloft" over the streets of Constantinople stands in direct opposition to the excitement I experienced in finding precisely that lofty view over the model of the *Kraton* in Yogyakarta. Disturbed by the uncanny resonance of these two traveling/architectural moments, separated as they are by 135 years and ten thousand odd kilometers, I decided to investigate further.

1. Herman Melville, *The Melville Log: A Documentary Life of Herman Melville 1819-1891* vol. 2, ed. Jay Leyda (New York: Gordian Press, 1969), 536.

Melville's complaints of "no plan to streets," "no numbers," "no names," culminate in exasperation, "no anything." The lack of any of the familiar codes culminated, for Melville, in a lack of "anything" at all; without the encoding mechanisms of street names, numbers, or maps, it was almost as if the city did not exist. In discussing colonial constructions of the idea of Egypt, Timothy Mitchell cites Melville's journal entry and reads his exasperation as a symptom of a more general nineteenth-century European conception of the world and of its relationship to the individual.[2] Mitchell describes this emergent conception as the world-as-exhibition, "a place where one was continually pressed into service as a spectator by a world ordered so as to represent."[3]

In his discussion of the world-as-exhibition Mitchell works from Martin Heidegger's essay "The Age of the World Picture."[4] For Heidegger, the modern age was characterized in terms of the pictorial, "the modern world picture [*Weltbild*]."[5] Heidegger used the words "world" and "picture" in very specific ways:

> Picture" here does not mean some imitation, but rather what sounds forth in the colloquial expression, "We get the picture" [literally, we are in the picture] concerning something.... "We get the picture" concerning something does not mean only that what is, is set before us, is represented to us, in general, but that what is stands before us—in all that belongs to it and all that stands together in it—as a system. "To get the picture" throbs with being acquainted with something, with being equipped and prepared for it. Where the world becomes picture, what is, in its entirety, is juxtaposed as that for which man is prepared and which, correspondingly, he therefore intends to bring before himself and have before himself, and consequently intends in a decisive sense to set in place before himself. Hence world picture, when understood essentially, does not mean a picture of the world but the world conceived and grasped as picture.[6]

The world-as-exhibition can be understood, then, in terms of representational equipment that is set to work in the preparation, conception and grasping of the world. The structure of this equipment is characterized as pictorial because of its ability to "set before us" and "represent to us" the world and, in doing so, to construct for us a subject "position" relative to that object world. "Now for the first time is there any such thing as a

2. Timothy Mitchell, *Colonising Egypt* (Cambridge: Cambridge University Press, 1988), 32.
3. Ibid., 13.
4. Martin Heidegger, "The Age of the World Picture," in *The Question Concerning Technology and Other Essays*, trans. William Lovitt (New York: Harper and Row, 1977), 115–54.
5. Ibid., 128.
6. Ibid., 129.

'position' of man."[7] This pictorial structure relies on the frame, and the screen it establishes, to intervene between the subject and the object worlds, to constitute both the viewer and the picture as it distinguishes between them. Subject and object effects vary with the specific formations and deployment of representational equipment, but in general it is possible to say that the structure of the frame and screen is the key mechanism that makes this operation possible. This is the case whether it be the bars on the animal cages at the zoo, the beading of the display case at the museum, the mullions of the department store window, the covers of the touristic guide book, or the picture plane of the projected drawing.

The effective operation of the world-as-exhibition, its ability to define and fix objective reality and subjective experience to produce a "reality effect," is founded on a logic of pictorial transparency. We are asked to see through the frame and screen to the reality and truth beyond; the representational equipment is understood to merely "facilitate" our view and so should not be allowed to "interfere" with the viewing. The apparently self-evident logic of this conception produces the "transparency" of the representational equipment: the representational nature of the frame and screen is masked as presentational. The effectiveness of this logic is such that Melville, when confronted by an environment that is not "ordered so as to represent," is profoundly disturbed. His disturbance is a symptom of a rupturing of the conditions upon which his own subjectivity as a spectator are founded. He is ill equipped in this unfamiliar space; he has no "position," "no anything."

Mitchell reworks Heidegger's question of being in the modern age into a more specific question of colonialism and its production in the modern age. Modernity and colonialism are intimately connected; indeed, it has been said, "the 'armed version' of modernism is colonialism itself."[8] It should also be noted that, historically, "the organization of world exhibitions coincided with the growth of European imperial confidence and power."[9] It was the sure and certain framing gaze of the spectator subject that claimed the "non-West" as its object of difference. Epistemological certainty underpinned the political confidence, which in turn underpinned the colonial project.

Returning for a moment to the two excerpts cited at the beginning of this essay, I could speculate that it was a model, map, picture, or some other piece of representational equipment that Melville felt he needed. This equipment, as noted above, is structured as frame and screen, and works by a mode of transparency to construct the

7. Ibid., 132.
8. Ashis Nandy cited in Stephen Slemon, "Modernism's Last Post," in *Past the Last Post*, ed. Ian Adam and Helen Tiffin (Calgary, Alta.: University of Calgary Press, 1990), 7.
9. Mitchell, *Colonizing Egypt*, 6.

subject "position" and an object world. This is perhaps the frame's most dangerous and, in the context of colonial productivity, most effective trait. My own excitement at discovering the model of the Yogyakarta *Kraton* complex was, I believe, driven by this same drive of modernity. The lure of the model was the lure of an object "set before us," framed for viewing, an object constituted by the distance it places between itself and the viewer. The frustration at my inability to clearly see the model, caused by the scratched and reflective surface of the Perspex that encased it, was driven by a desire for a screen of pure and literal transparency. It was the return of this colonial productivity—so apparent in the nineteenth-century context Melville describes—within the structure of my own architectural questions that I found uncanny and disturbing.

These drives have long been embedded within the architectural institution, and as long as the representational equipment that architecture employs in the face of other "architecture" remains "self-evident," the colonial productivity of its transparency will persist. According to Homi Bhabha "the discourses and institutions of literature [and we may add architecture here] can only provide a dim and refracted light that casts a shadow on an alien culture."[10] Despite (and because of) the best intentions of sensitive, enlightened scholarship, the representational equipment of this modern institution continues to haunt the various scenes of cross-cultural negotiation in a shadowy form. The modern (and colonial) promise of a clear, even light of epistemological certainty seems unfounded. Cross-cultural negotiation can no longer be a case of rendering representational equipment ever more transparent or its light ever brighter in an attempt to mask the shadowy nature of its productivity. Yet to declare this logic to be redundant does little in itself to disrupt the power of its productivity. Rather, tactics for a disruption of this kind are more likely to be found in an investigation of the condition of the shadow and its modes of production. In the remainder of this essay I would like to return to the Yogyakarta *Kraton* complex, the architectural object of my journal entry, and examine it more carefully in these terms.

The Indo-European Style Debate

The figure of the *Kraton* was raised, with some ambivalence, on the fringes of architectural discourse in the Dutch East Indies in the 1920s. This discourse took the form of a debate that was underpinned by the notion of a moral obligation on part of the

10. Homi K. Bhabha, "Representation and the Colonial Text: A Critical Exploration of Some Forms of Mimeticism," in *The Theory of Reading*, ed. Frank Gloversmith (Brighton: Harvester Press, 1984), 95.

architect to produce an "architecture of the age" and "of the Indies." The development of this attitude is exemplified, as early as 1914, by S. Sniujff, an engineer in the Public Works Department of the colonial government:

> No national colonial architecture exists at present even after 3 centuries during which the Dutch were established in the East.... mild climate and the fertility of the soil have never created anxiety on the part of the uncivilized population to acquire better or more permanent dwellings.[11]

Indigenous populations, without the necessary anxiety, were seen to be incapable of producing an architecture that would embody new social and cultural values. The new values of the Indies were understood as developing out of a hybrid of European and indigenous cultures, and were to be articulated architecturally as the "Indo-European style." The aesthetic, philosophical, and institutional means for the development of an Indo-European architecture were debated specifically in a series of lectures and more generally in the press throughout the 1920s. Experimental design projects for exhibitions and annual fairs were conducted to test for architectural hybrid vigor. The founding assumption of the debate was that the hybrid nature of the new style would require some indigenous architectural substance with which to cross European architectural strains. The debate, spurred by an emergent "ethical" sentiment, reinforced and gave new impetus to existing cultural salvage projects that had developed in the context of archaeological discourse in the colony. While a common ethical sentiment was implicitly shared by advocates of different positions within the debate, a primary point of contention arose around the question of which indigenous architecture should serve as the founding model. Two lines of argument emerged: the first position was most forcefully put by Wolff Schoemaker, Professor of Architecture at the Technical High School in Bandung, West Java. He argued,

> the Indies d[o] not have an architecture tradition.... Old forms are often no longer suitable to satisfy the practical and spiritual needs, anyway, so far as one can say about indigenous building methods. Architecture in the sense that it has for us does not exist in Java.[12]

The old forms referred to here are the wooden pavilion forms found specifically in villages and towns throughout rural Java. These forms represented, for Schoemaker, "the degenerate, declined-to-nothing Javanese art of building in wood."[13] At the very most,

11. S. Sniujff, cited in Iwan Sudrajat, "Indonesian Architectural History," Ph.D. Dissertation, University of Sydney, 1991, 159.
12. Wolff Schoemaker, cited in Helen Ibbitson Jessup, "Netherlands Architecture in Indonesia, 1900–42," Ph.D. Dissertation, Courtauld Institute of Art, University of London, 1989, 132. For much of the material on the Indo-European style debate I have relied on Jessup's invaluable thesis.
13. Ibid., 134.

he conceded this art of building held an "embryonic" architectural status.[14] The "degenerate" nature of Javanese building correlated with an inherent Javanese racial "decadence":

> [Javanese, with] infantile impotence [and]...naive spiritual expressions [were capable of producing only]...soulless, manually-laboured art [and]...senseless, dry copying...[and shared] only their skin colour and a few of the qualities caused by tropical nature with the more highly anthropologically-developed races of the East.[15]

Schoemaker is referring to Indians when he speaks of "the more highly anthropologically-developed races of the East"; he had no hesitation in ascribing the building traditions of India a full and mature architectural status. These Indian traditions, he argued, were exemplified in Java by *candi* structures of the eighth and ninth centuries at Borobudur and Prambanan. Both *candi* structures exhibit overt Indian influences in terms of form, technique, and ornament, and were assumed to have been constructed under direct supervision of Indian expertise. It was on this foundation, imported from India, indubitably architectural in nature, that a new Indo-European tradition could be established. Schoemaker's vision was founded on the hybridizing of two "great civilizations," Europe and India, and the transplanting of this hybrid into the mild climate and fertile soil of Java.

The second position in the debate for a foundational indigenous architecture was argued by Thomas Karsten and Henri Maclaine Pont. Their position was supported by the Dutch architect H. P. Berlage, whose arrival in the Indies in 1923 intensified the debate. They saw the ancient "Indian" architectural tradition as "alien" to existing indigenous traditions and as irrelevant to contemporary life in the Indies. The "Indian" architectural tradition, they argued, had to be rejected as a basis for contemporary architectural development. Karsten and Maclaine Pont argued that "Indian" architectural principles could not be adapted to contemporary spatial requirements.

> The proper basis for the further development of native architecture...is to be found in "living architecture," that is, in late Javanese architecture, which still relates to the ancient art but for some centuries has developed into an independent style. The artistic capacity of this architectural tradition

14. Wolff Schoemaker, cited in Sudrajat, "Indonesian Architectural History," 172.
15. Wolff Schoemaker, cited in Jessup, *Netherlands Architecture in Indonesia*, 134.

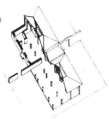

Javanese house from
the Jogjakarta region
1
axonometric
2
sectional drawing
showing, left to right,
the *pendapa*, *pring-
gitan*, and *dalem*

is particularly evident in the "pendopo" [*pendapa*] type of building, which found its climax in the *Kraton*.[16]

It is here, in Karsten and Maclaine Pont's argument that the figure of the *Kraton* first occurs in architectural discourse. The *Kraton pendapa* was the "highest" manifestation of the Javanese "art of building in wood." Karsten and Maclaine Pont, backed by Berlage, argued for its elevation into the status of "architecture," while Schoemaker, conceding that it may be an "embryonic" form of architecture, maintained that it was essentially "building."

I should pause at this point to briefly describe this pivotal *Kraton pendapa* building, or architecture, reserving judgment for the moment on the relative merits of the two lines of argument that circulate around it.

The most important spatial arrangement in the *Kraton* occurs at its center, where three key pavilions—the *pendapa*, the *pringgitan*, and the *dalem*—are located. Together the three pavilions are usually referred to as the "Javanese house" (figs. 1 and 2). The arrangement of these three pavilions is an arrangement that structures traditional housing throughout many villages of rural Java. The pavilions are structurally and formally independent but are held together in tension by an axis threaded through them. The *pendapa* and the *dalem* are very similar in form and structure; each is almost square in plan, and each has a central structural core that supports a high pyramidal roof. Spatially, however, the two pavilions are fundamentally different. The *pendapa* is traditionally not enclosed in any way: it is light, open, public, and perhaps considered more profane. The *dalem*, on the other hand, is wrapped in a brick, timber or woven bamboo screen that completely encloses the space: it is dark, enclosed, private and—because of its central cell or "hearth"—could be considered sacred. Y. B. Mangunwijaya has described the *pendapa* as being the "umbrella in the courtyard" and the *dalem* as the "cave."[17]

Mediating between the *pendapa* and the *dalem* is the *pringgitan*. It is the least visible of the forms that constitute "the Javanese house," having the same width of the other pavilions, but having a depth between one and a half and two meters and a roof that is relatively low and unspectacular. The *pringgitan* form is so shallow that, as one moves through from the *pendapa* to the *dalem*, it is barely perceptible as a separate space. Mangunwijaya describes the *pringgitan* as the line (*garis*) between the *pendapa* and the *dalem*.[18]

16. Thomas Karsten and Henri Maclaine Pont, cited in Sudrajat, "Indonesian Architectural History," 164.
17. Y. B. Mangunwijaya, *Wastu Citra: Pengantar ke Ilmu Budaya Arsitektur Sendi-sendi Filsfatnya Beserta Contoh-contoh Praktis* (Jakarta: Gramedia Pustaka Utama, 1992), 106, translated by the author.
18. Ibid.

For Karsten and Maclaine Pont it was the *pendapa* form, the *Kraton pendapa* in particular, that underpinned their argument for a hybrid Indo-European architecture. That they should have focused so intently on the *pendapa* form is, in many ways, not surprising. Without the cladding or any of the "extraneous" cells of the *dalem*, the *pendapa* can be seen as a clear unified expression of structure and form. The elegance of the roof as it sweeps down to approach the horizontal, the ballast of the structural core over four central columns, the gentle bending of the rafters as they radiate from this center, and the way the roof casts shade in the hot courtyard are all features of the *pendapa* form that have been noted over the years in architectural writing. It is not surprising that the Dutch architectural scholars focused on the *pendapa*, as the *pendapa* continues to appeal to contemporary architectural sensibilities. In its formal, structural, and functional unity, the *pendapa* performs as a "natural" object of architecture, and in this way it continues to make architectural sense.

The position articulated and defended most notably by Karsten, Maclaine Pont, and Berlage has been most influential for contemporary regionalist discourse dealing with Indonesian architecture. The overtly racist position that Schoemaker constructed is easily dismissed in the face of concerns for the local and the indigenous. As a consequence it is the *Kraton* form typified by the *pendapa*, augmented with an attention to factual conditions of local climate, local materials, and function, that has come to dominate contemporary discussions.

The kind of negotiations that were conducted over "the art of building in wood" in the Indo-European style and their subsequent elaboration in contemporary regionalist architectural discourse need to be examined closely precisely because the form and outcome of those negotiations continue to make sense so effortlessly. Great effort is usually required to sustain the effect of effortlessness; a complex battery of equipment is required for its production—equipment, that is, that maximizes the effort to disavow the effect of effort. This equipment and the modes of its deployment need to be considered. What kind of equipment is required to support the category "traditional Javanese architecture"? What kind of equipment is required for that "architecture" to "make sense"? And further, what kind of equipment is required to mask the labor of such equipment?

In attempting to open a space in which these questions might be answered, I will focus on two moments of repression that can be read from the brief account of the Indo-European debate given above. Both of these involve representational equipment that take the form of frame, screen, and projected shadow.

Architectural Repressions

Karsten, Maclaine Pont, and Berlage (and others since) have succeeded in claiming an architectural status for the *pendapa* form. This has been achieved by the careful, sensitive, and detailed research conducted on traditional wooden buildings in Java and by their assessment in terms of architectural criteria of formal, structural, and functional appropriateness.

The pivotal implement for such architectural research is the idea of drawing. Through drawing architectural practice is able to take on the form of "autonomous and abstract creation."[19] It is said in classical mythology that drawing was invented by the tracing of a figure's cast shadow. Robin Evans considered two instances of this primordial scenario's representation in art and saw the possibility of two quite different kinds of drawing.[20] The first assumes a lamp to be the source of light for the tracing, and the second assumes it to be the sun. The point source of the lamp projects light in the form of a cone; this principle, when mirrored along the line of the image surface by another conical projection converging on the retina of an eye, describes the perspective construction. Etymologically, the term "perspective" implies a seeing through. The surface onto which the shadow is cast could be reconceived as the screen through which the viewing subject sees; the viewer is then an integral part of the construction, conceptually always present. In the second possibility, the diffused light of the sun denies the conical geometry; light in this instance is more akin to a series of parallel rays without a single origin. This principle, when mirrored along the line of the image surface by another set of parallel projections onto a conceptual all-seeing eye, describes the orthographic projection. The all-seeing eye is an idealized eye that maintains an orthogonal relationship with every point of the picture plane. In this way orthographic projection is seen to correct distortions of perspective projection. In both instances the trajectory of light is interrupted by an object and casts a shadow onto a surface; this is then traced to produce the image. But the

19. Helene Lipstadt, "Architectural Publication, Competitions and Exhibitions," *Architecture and its Image: Four Centuries of Architectural Representation*, ed. Eve Blau and Edward Kaufman (Cambridge, MA: MIT Press, 1989), 109.
20. Robin Evans, "Translations from Drawing to Building," *AA Files* 12 (1986): 6.

different sources of this light give the first an artistic relative value and the second a scientific one. As the perspective projection is contingent on a single point of view, it implies a more intimate, subjective, and artistic representation. The orthographic projection, with an infinite number of correct views, suggests accurate, objective, and scientific representation. As Evans was concerned specifically with architectural production, he aligned perspective more closely with art, and orthographic projection with architecture. Yet, in claiming institutional identity as mediator between material and intellectual worlds, architecture relies on both forms of projection.

These different modes of drawing systematically construct different "positions" by which the modern subject is able to "bring," to "have," to "place before himself" the world. By exploiting the two possibilities of these drawing modes architecture gives itself a "position" at which to stand, a specific institutional subjectivity that is at once intimate and distant, at once artistic and scientific. In this exploitation, however, architecture in turn relies on the logic of the frame and screen, and of the shadow. The construction of a stable position of architectural subject is dependent on the paradigm of the fickle and insubstantial. The shadow is required, but only insofar as its insubstantial nature can be made substantial, its fickleness fixed in the process of tracing. Tracing constructs an image that is productive in and for architecture. In the manner of that ethnographic phantasm, that participant/observer—able, at once, to intimately share a common human experience and to stand back and observe dispassionately—architectural researchers work to carefully construct their object to very precise institutional specifications. The construction of a specific combination of views can be seen as a process of translating into the architectural language, a language that has pretensions of universality. What is fundamentally different is rendered the same by the ability of this translation to construct an image of exchangeability.

This process of architectural translation occurred in Java in the preparations for a series of architectural exhibitions. Henri Maclaine Pont was involved in planning the first of these, held in Semarang on the north coast of Java in 1914, planned in part as a catalyst for a housing development on the outskirts of the city. The exhibition was to establish a basic infrastructure for the development, such as roads, transportation, and a water supply, and to generate an interest in the idea of living outside of the old city center.

The development was motivated in part by the colonial authority's concern for the falling standards of public health due to overcrowding in the city, and in part by private sector concerns for increasing land values outside the city. But for Maclaine Pont this exhibition was "above all the first big expression of the Netherlands Indies as one indivisible nation."[21] The governmental and private sector agendas for the exhibition were refigured in Maclaine Pont's mind: for him the exhibition was an expression of cultural difference and of an Indo-European identity.

Maclaine Pont was responsible for the overall site planning and the design of a number of exhibition structures. The exhibition as a whole was to consist of two sections, an indigenous section and a European section, while the exhibition structures themselves were planned to display local handicrafts, art objects from the Yogyakarta (and Solo) *Kraton*, and archaeological finds; craftsmen were to be installed in recreated village settings to produce works on site. Most interesting for the purposes of this argument, however, is that a "gamelan house," "*wayang* [shadow puppet] tents" (both treated as autonomous cultural performances, to be accommodated separately from equally autonomous architectural artifacts), and a "series of magnificent Indonesian houses from the outer islands" and from various parts of Java were planned. Maclaine Pont refers specifically to the "tensile-roofed houses" from parts of Sumatra, Bali, and Java as "those beautiful buildings," and continues,

> With the design of the first general plan of the exhibition, the idea of bringing west and east together without suppressing either has been in the foreground.... Some typical differences between the architecture of the modern western and that of the eastern people were to have been expressed.[22]

For Maclaine Pont the exhibition was created to express cultural difference and an Indo-European identity. In reading his descriptions of the project it becomes clear that Maclaine Pont understood this "difference" and "identity" to be best expressed in specifically architectural terms. It was in architecture—in the hybridized "beautiful buildings" of the various cultures of the colony—that cultural difference and an Indo-European identity could be found. One of those "beautiful, tensile-roofed buildings" would have been the Javanese *pendapa*.

83   21. Henri Maclaine Pont cited in Jessup, *Netherlands Architecture in Indonesia*, 209.
22. Ibid., 211–12.

3
Scene from *wayang*
performance

4
The private side of
wayang performance

Only the European section of the exhibition was completed, much to Maclaine Pont's disappointment. Nonetheless the design work that he undertook involved drawing the exhibition site plan and the arrangement of the architectural exhibits. This activity of drawing—of conscious reflection—was intimately connected to the planning and implementation of the Semarang exhibition. It represented the beginning of a process of architectural research, which was elaborated by the annual Pasar Gambir fair in Jakarta, the first of which was held in 1921. These annual fairs became an important media through which the Indo-European style debate was articulated publicly; they were places where architects could design and build their "explorations" of various indigenous built forms.[23]

It was through drawing that Maclaine Pont began to translate the *pendapa* as architecture. This translation produced a different architecture, but different only insofar as it could operate within the frame of the museum, the exhibition, the journal, or, more generally, the architectural institution. Constructed in this way, as object to be viewed, the *pendapa* was made available for "exploration" and "experimentation" in the representational world of the Pasar Gambir fair.

The success of this mobilization can be seen in the ease with which the position put by Schoemaker has been more recently dismissed by regionalist and nationalist architectural discourse. What is repressed in this triumph of the colonial policy of "ethical" cultural administration are certain possibilities of difference activated by "the Javanese art of building in wood"; these are traits that are domesticated by the elevation of "building" to "architecture," by the inclusion of the *pendapa* form within the institutional frame of architecture. In his refusal to consider the *Kraton* or any other *pendapa* as architecture, Schoemaker inadvertently provided a space for the construction of an architecture of radical difference, an architecture that never simply took its place within the frame of an architectural discourse. It was this potentially ambivalent space and this threat of difference that Karsten, Maclaine Pont, Berlage, and others nullified.

The great effort to mobilize this complex institutional equipment was matched only by the effort to disavow its mobilization. The equipment that Karsten, Maclaine Pont, and Berlage disavow is the frame and screen of architectural research. In the light of their scholarly gaze can be picked an elegant silhouette of architectural form that casts architectural projections, flat and shadowlike, yet traceable and infinitely

23. Sudrajat, "Indonesian Architectural History," 162.

5
Wayang puppets

6
Wayang performance

translatable. The *pendapa* is not inherently architectural; rather its architectural status is negotiated, ascribed, and, consequently fetishized as a structurally elegant, beautiful object. Its object status is projected and drawn out of the opacities it presents to the architectural light cast on to it. Only in this objectlike state does the *pendapa* make architectural sense.

Thus an Indo-European identity is claimed by architectural means; in doing so architecture's own institutional identity is reaffirmed. This move is made according to specific institutional specifications that, in establishing rules for inclusion, must inevitably mark exclusions. If, as I have argued, the *pendapa* form is included into the frame of architecture according to specifications of structural, functional, and formal appropriateness, what exclusions do these specifications imply? If the *pendapa* is included to make architectural sense, what is excluded and left to make architectural non-sense?

The answer may be found in another part of the "Javanese house." As mentioned above, a low, narrow, and unspectacular form mediates between the two principle pavilions in the center of the Yogyakarta *Kraton*. This least visible form is the *pringgitan*. The term *pringgitan* is derived from "*ringgit*," which is an Old Javanese word meaning "*wayang*," literally shadow; "*wayang*" also describes the culture of the Javanese shadow play—the puppets, the stories, and the performance. The *pringgitan* is the place where the screen traditionally is located for a *wayang* performance. A large frame is set up here across which a white screen is stretched. Located in the *pendapa* is a lamp that casts light onto flat puppets that in turn cast shadows onto the screen (fig. 3). Also in the *pendapa* are the *dalang*, or puppeteer, and the gamelan orchestra (fig. 4). From this private side the *wayang* puppets, cut out of flat buffalo hide and intricately carved and painted with rich color, are visible (fig. 5). The shadows cast by the *wayang* puppets are only visible from inside the *dalem*. From this public side the painted color of the *wayang* puppets is not visible. The *wayang* puppet forms are destabilized by the way they are manipulated in front of the light source on the other side of the screen; their original scales and proportions are distorted (fig. 6).

The various manifestations of the Indo-European style debate do not make immediately apparent the place of the *pringgitan* and the particular frame, screen, and shadow structure of *wayang*. Of the various components of the Javanese house it is the *pringgitan* that remains most blatantly undrawn, unexhibited, unphotographed, undiscussed. This is not surprising: the *pringgitan* is, after all, the least visible form—structurally and formally unspectacular, functionally non-sensical—and the *wayang* structure it houses simply marks the space between the *pendapa* and the *dalem*. If the *pendapa* is included to make architectural sense, the *pringgitan* is excluded and left to make architectural non-sense. What institutional specifications mark the *pringgitan* as non-sense? Why should its exclusion make sense and not be surprising?

This question may be augmented by considering an argument put by nineteenth-century architectural theorist Gottfried Semper. (If the intrusion of the figure of Semper into the discussion at this point seems strange, it should be noted that Semper's teaching was formatively influential on the thinking of Berlage, who, as I noted earlier, played an influential role in the Indo-European style debate in Java in the 1920s.) Semper argues that the origins of architecture are found in the use of woven fabrics.

The weaving of branches led easily to weaving bast into mats and covers and then to weaving with plant fiber and so forth. . . . Hanging carpets remained the true walls, the visible boundaries of space. The often solid walls behind them were necessary for reasons that had nothing to do with the creation of space; they were needed for security, for supporting a load, for their permanence, and so on. Wherever the need for these secondary functions did not arise, the carpets remained the original means of separating space. Even where building solid walls became necessary, the latter were only the inner, invisible structure hidden behind the true and legitimate representatives of the wall, the colorful woven carpets.[24]

The woven fabric is inherently patterned and ornamental, and yet, according to Semper, is primary in architecture: the tectonic and structural concerns of architecture are ascribed a secondary status.

For Karsten, Maclaine Pont, Berlage, and their followers, the *pringgitan* registers as the least significant of the three forms of the "Javanese house." In its linearity the *pringgitan* has almost no three-dimensional presence; it almost escapes representational form. Yet for Semper this non-space would perhaps be the prime Javanese spatial gesture. In many ways it is the *wayang* screen—the line of the *pringgitan*—that distinguishes inside from outside, private from public, dark from light; almost all of the

24. Gottfried Semper, *The Four Elements of Architecture and Other Writings*, trans. Harry Francis Mallgrave and Wolfgang Herrmann (Cambridge: Cambridge University Press, 1989), 103.

spatial distinctions in the "Javanese house" are set in play by the frame and screen housed in the *pringgitan*. If the *pringgitan* is non-space, then the power of its spatial gesture is in its two-dimensionality, which takes the form of the translucent, ornamental, and woven surface of the *wayang* screen and the flat *wayang* puppets that occupy it.

The role of the *pringgitan* and *wayang* as "the true and legitimate representative of the wall [as] colorful woven carpet" is primary. Yet this notion of ornamental primacy was not an issue in the Indo-European style debate, and it remains a relatively minor concern in subsequent regionalist architectural agendas. This returns us to the question of the role this ornamental surface plays in the institutional specifications of architecture, which can be explored by considering Semper's location within those specifications.

There is a long history in architectural discourse of maintaining a structure-ornament hierarchy in which structure is the primary and foundational term and ornament the secondary and supplemental. Semper's argument was controversial precisely because it disturbed this hierarchy by inverting its order: ornament is given a primary and foundational role, while structure is understood as a kind of temporary scaffolding. In his discussion of this controversy, Mark Wigley argued that Semper posed a threat to the traditional structure of architectural discourse, such that it became necessary to repress the ornamental primacy for which he argued.

> The resistance to Semper is therefore symptomatic. It takes more the form of repression than rejection. His work is not so much written out of the institutional discourse as buried within it. It is swallowed, neither to be digested nor to be thrown up.[25]

> Sigmund Freud contended, "The essence of repression lies simply in turning something away, and keeping it at a distance from the unconscious."[26] This action of "keeping it at a distance" carries with it the implication that that which has been turned away could return. It is this ambivalent state, something swallowed yet neither digested nor thrown up, that distinguishes repression from rejection.

The repression of Semper's argument suggests that the ornamental surface of the *wayang* in the *pringgitan* was, and continues to be, problematic for an architecture specified as fundamentally tectonic. The frame, screen, and shadow of the *wayang* do not securely fix an image and a position for the viewing of that image in a mutually confirming

25. Mark Wigley, "Untitled: The Housing of Gender," *Sexuality and Space*, ed. Beatriz Colomina (New York: Princeton Architectural Press, 1992), 373.

26. Sigmund Freud, *The Standard Edition of the Complete Psychological Works* vol. 14 (London: Hogarth Press, 1953), 147.

subject-object relationship. The shadows of the *wayang* screen do not operate within the principles of accuracy and translatability. As the *wayang* shadows are cast onto the screen, their forms act in accordance with the motives of the *dalang*. As the *wayang* themselves press against the screen they become sharply defined silhouettes, and as they are lifted away form the screen surface their images distort, twist, and warp. The "vanishing point" of the lamp explodes and diffuses the image rather than drawing it towards unity; the structure of the *wayang* seems to operate outside the representational structure of the dichotomy between subject "position" and object world.

In the drive to produce the functional, structural, and formal appropriateness of the *pendapa*, the flat, ornamental, and insubstantial nature of the *wayang* is repressed. As the inevitability of the shadow in its own structure is repressed, so too the role of the shadow in the drawing of the Javanese house is repressed.

Re-surfacing

Nineteenth-century colonial arguments continue to structure many aspects of the regionalist question despite the resistance to or criticism of these arguments inherent to the question's formation. We cannot escape these discursive conditions of the architectural institution; there is no other, more authentic, originary space outside of these conditions. The "Javanese house" is brought into the fringes of this institution and made architectural by the various lines of argument Schoemaker, Karsten, Maclaine Pont, Berlage, and many others weave around it. If there is no authentic space outside this fabricated condition then another space of resistance must be constructed from within its weave. The refusal of Schoemaker to concede the "Javanese house" the status of architecture opens one such space. From this kind of space—a space within the boundaries of architectural discourse—the threat of an architecture of radical difference can be reconceived. The form of this radical difference is, paradoxically, almost formless: the two-dimensional ornamental surface of the *wayang* screen and the *wayang* puppets that occupy it. The difference posited here does not emerge from an authentic condition indigenous to Java. Rather, it is a difference that emerges at the intersection of architectural discourse and its other. In this way, perhaps, a reconsideration of that pivotal *wayang* surface in the "Javanese house" may lead to a re-surfacing of an architectural threat hitherto kept in check.

88   I am grateful to Karen Burns, Philippa Moylan, and Gülsüm Baydar Nalbantoğlu for their careful readings and critiques of earlier versions of this paper.

Limits of (in)Tolerance: The Carved Dwelling in the Architectural and Urban Discourse of Modern Turkey
Gülsüm Baydar Nalbantoğlu

The cave, the cavern, and the carved dwelling have a long history in Western architectural discourse as the basis of an entire narrative of origins. Theorists from Vitruvius to the Enlightenment named the cave the most archaic form of shelter, representing a state of savagery. According to the Vitruvian narrative it took countless generations to evolve from the cave to the hut. The former is pure interior, structureless and invisible; it defies proper architectural analysis and conventional technologies of representation. The latter is constructed, visible, and objectifiable. Architectural truth has come to mean leaving the cave behind.[1] At one level, the irreconcilable differences between these two prototypes can be linked to a family of binary constructions that lies at the basis of the architectural discipline: nature/culture, vernacular/high-style, rural/urban, and traditional/modern. At another level, however, the inhabited cave has an ambiguous status. It lies at the significatory boundary of architecture rather than simply falling outside. It is neither "natural" nor "man-made," both inhabitable and impossible to objectify.[2] The inhabited cave is located at the border of architecture's grand narrative, which is inscribed by a desire for the autonomy of immortal architectural objects.

Along this line of thinking, I was captivated by three very different scenes that mark the history of the carved dwelling in Turkish architectural discourse. In these instances the intriguing status of the carved dwelling in Western architectural discourse is further complicated by the cultural status of Turkish architecture on the fringes of such discourse where, like in all postcolonial encounters, meanings are contested, negotiated, reinterpreted, and transformed.[3] Hence the three historical scenes raise two significant issues. On one hand they demonstrate certain repressions involved in the construction of proper architectural discourse. They are reminders that architecture, like all disciplines, continuously defers any interrogation of its externality. It draws boundaries, erects walls, controls openings, and guards its foundations. On the other hand, they show that architecture's disciplinary inclusions and exclusions and their modes of legitimation are historically and contextually inscribed. These issues are rarely theorized outside a disciplinary

All translations by Gülsüm Baydar Nalbantoğlu, unless otherwise noted.

1. Plato used the mythological scene of a cave to build the deeply influential notion of a self-identical idea that belongs to the realm of a pure unchanging Being. In a powerful critique of Plato's metaphor, Luce Irigaray points to the fact that in his scenario of the three scenes—i.e., the cave, the world, and the ideas—there is an implicit division of labor between the intelligible and its material and sensible conditions of existence. Truth has come to mean leaving behind the cave (the sensible) and its role in production. My account here is largely inspired by her interpretation. See Luce Irigaray, *Speculum of the Other Woman* (New York: Cornell University Press, 1985), 243–364; Margaret Whitford, *Luce Irigaray: Philosophy in the Feminine* (London: Routledge, 1991), 105–13.
2. I would argue that, once inhabited, the cave disrupts the natural/man-made opposition regardless

1
The carved town
of Uçhisar in
Cappadocia

desire to incorporate the unfamiliar either by an unabashed assertion of Eurocentric hegemony or by a humanistic celebration of cultural/ architectural diversity. The former position perpetuates the hegemonic drives that underlie the binary constructions of East/West, culture/civilization, and vernacular/high style. The latter avoids all questions of incommensurability and radical difference. The violence involved in the construction of the very boundaries of the discipline is rarely acknowledged.

The different cases of the carved dwelling in Turkish architectural discourse attracted me because of my interest in the mechanisms of legitimation in architecture, and in the operation of modernist architectural discourses outside the West. Like the grand narratives of many postcolonial cultures, that of modern Turkish architecture has been inscribed by two seemingly opposed pedagogies of nativism and international modernism.[4] The former involves the study of rural, regional, indigenous buildings. The latter looks to contemporary Western models. Both exclude any critical analysis of view of urban encounters with rural Turkey. These encounters, I would argue, are sites of resistance and subversion as much as assimilation and domestication. The carved dwelling is significant in Turkish architectural discourse as its ambiguous architectural status allows it a special place within this context.

First Scene: Naming

In 1933, Abdullah Ziya, an architect with the Turkish Ministry of Education in Ankara, classified Turkish villages into two topographical groups: villages in mountainous areas and villages in the plains.[5] Each category consisted of sub-categories based on building materials available in different regions. Similar to many regionalists, Ziya was fascinated by the ingenious use of local materials and techniques. There was one category, however, for which he had no words of praise. What he called "negative villages" consisted of houses that were carved into rocky mountains (fig. 1). "When you look at these villages from afar," he reported, "you see numerous people wiggling in the cavities of the porous mountain." He concluded that since the negative villages did "not have any formal or aesthetic merit," he did "not find it necessary to write about them at length."

Abdullah Ziya's article appeared in *Ülkü*, an important journal whose mission was to educate the Turkish population along the lines of modernizing reforms in civic life. As extensively studied by historians, the early years of the Turkish republic were

of the seeming distinction between a naturally formed cave and a carved dwelling. The "naturalness" of the former is challenged by the first physical traces of inhabitation, such as drawings on the walls; the latter, on the other hand, often consists of enlargements of existing caves formed on soft rocky terrain. In tracing the origin of the dwelling, Vitruvius attributes inferior status to both the cave and the carved dwelling in comparison to the hut. Vitruvius, *The Ten Books on Architecture*, trans. Morris Hicky Morgan (New York: Dover, 1960), 38.

3. I use the term "postcolonial" rather loosely here. In the late phases of the Ottoman Empire colonization took place at the economic and cultural levels rather than in the form of direct political domination. For a classic work on the economic rights and privileges granted to foreign nations and the cultural transformations in the nineteenth and twentieth centuries, see Stanford J. Shaw and Ezel Kural Shaw,

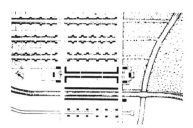

2
Burhan Arif, plan
for a model village,
1935

marked by a monumental project of cultural modernization.[6] Often characterized as
"modernization from above," it involved a series of educational, legal, and cultural reforms
that were instigated to cut all the links with the country's Ottoman and Islamic past. The
reformation of the countryside was a significant component of this project. The 1930s and
early 1940s saw unprecedented efforts not only in the accumulation and systematization of
data on rural Turkey but also in the realization of the republic's civilizing mission in many
rural settlements. In architectural terms, these attempts took the form of a series of built
and unbuilt ideal types ranging from model villages to individual houses. These were
inspired by a host of Western examples including German *Siedlungs* and *Existenzminimum*
housing principles (fig. 2). Model villages consisted of neatly arranged rows of identical
houses, reminiscent of the disciplinary environments of nineteenth-century factory towns.
Typical rural houses were designed as miniaturized versions of urban apartments. The
bodies to inhabit these ideal schemes were to be ideal bodies equipped with signs of
civility. As one architect put it, the mission was "to introduce beds to those who are used to
sleeping together on earthen floors, to teach how to use chairs to those who sit on the floor,
to provide tables for those who eat on the floors, to revolutionize lifestyles."[7] It would
obviously be difficult to incorporate any existing Turkish village into such ideal visions.
Typological studies were done, however, mostly to study climatic and topographical effects,
which would then be incorporated into new proposals.

    Why then, were the negative villages found of no architectural merit, and,
more importantly perhaps, how were they expelled from Abdullah Ziya's discourse? The
answer to the first question seems quite straightforward. As an architect educated in the
Western tradition, Abdullah Ziya's comments expressed the horror of the modernist vision at
the uncanny appearance of the carved dwelling in a (projected) modern context. I am more
interested, however, in how the moment of expulsion was symbolized. The expression,
"numerous people wiggling in the cavities of the porous mountain" unmistakably resonates
with a kind of repugnance. Yet it is the only instance in the article (if not in the entire discourse on Turkish rural architecture of the time) when the "bodies" that inhabit architecture
enter the architect's scope of vision. And the architect observes movement; the bodies are
"wiggling." Paradoxically, however, when bodies become visible to the architect, architecture
disappears from his vision. In Abdullah Ziya's discourse, structure and skin, the founding

91   *History of the Ottoman Empire and Modern Turkey* vol. 2 (London: Cambridge University Press, 1977).
    4. I have argued elsewhere that both of these pedagogies search for a center, ultimately a nationalist
core, that dissolves all forms of difference. Hence they mark the desire for a moment of transcen-
dence when the nostalgia for lost origins and the demand to civilize reveal themselves as two sides of
the same coin. See Gülsüm Baydar Nalbantoğlu, "Silent Interruptions: Urban Encounters with Rural
Turkey" in *Re-thinking the Modern Project in Turkey*, ed. Sibel Bozdoğan and Reşat Kasaba (Seattle:
Washington University Press, 1997).
    5. Abdullah Ziya, "Köy Mimarisi" (Village architecture), *Ülkü* vol. 1, no. 5 (June 1933): 370–74.
    6. For a recent collection of essays on this issue see Bozdoğan and Kasaba, *Re-thinking the Modern.*
    7. Zeki Sayar, "İç Kolonizasyon" (Colonization Inside), *Arkitekt* vol. 6, no. 2 (1936): 47.

3
Abdullah Ziya,
drawing of a village
located in a
mountainous area

elements of architecture that are absent in the carved dwelling, have collapsed into flesh. For all the other rural categories in his article, his descriptions are limited to pure form: the location of the village square, house forms, and building materials (fig. 3). Only the negative villages, "which have no formal or aesthetic merit," make inhabitation visible to him. The architect's eye does not desire inhabitation unless it is fully controlled/contained by architecture.

Jennifer Bloomer states in a different context that, in the history of architecture, One can find an ever-thickening entanglement of propriety centered on the body of beauty, a flight from the voluptuous: from the irrational, from the irregular, from the ornamental/supplemental, from the unrefined, from the uncut. . . . a construction that allows a certain "safe" distancing, made to the specifications of beauty. This is a distance that avoids the breath and the smell and the heat of fertile flesh, and thereby also avoids any reminder of mortality, of death.[8]

Flesh, as the reminder of death, has to be kept at a safe distance, out of vision. The death of flesh/body marks the birth of form/architecture. Abdullah Ziya captured the essence of this logic when he compared modernist cultural reform movements to the Turkish War of Independence. He wrote passionately that "the artistic aspect of the revolution, too, is a battle. This battle has to be fought by the young Turk. His knowledge, faith, and tireless and continuous diligence will lead to victory in this front as well."[9] The War of Independence was fought against other nations. But what about this one? Why the metaphor of warfare? War against whom? Questions multiply. I would argue that Abdullah Ziya's denial of architectural status to the "negative dwellings" is an extreme instance of a logic of destruction that governed the construction of the national (architectural) narrative of modern Turkey. The carved dwellings of the "negative villages" were rendered invisible by Ziya's desire to construct ideal types to house "civilized" bodies different than the "wiggling" bodies that obstructed the foreground of his perspective. Proper architecture could only be created by the destruction of the latter.

Second Scene: Assimilation

In the first scene, the carved dwelling was rendered proper architecture's other and excluded from the territorial claims of the discipline. As Helene Cixous put it,

8. Jennifer Bloomer, "... and Venustas," *AA Files* 25 (Summer 1993): 7.
9. Abdullah Ziya, "Cumhuriyette Köy Yapımı," (Village Building During the Republic) *Ülkü* vol. 2, no. 8 (September 1933): 334.

4
Murat Akok, axono-
metric drawing of
Kaymakli

The paradox of otherness is that, of course, at no moment in History is it
tolerated or possible as such. The other is there only to be reappropriated,
recaptured, and destroyed as other. . . . the body of what is strange must not
disappear, but its force must be conquered and returned to the master.[10]

If the carved dwelling was "destroyed" by Abdullah Ziya's discourse, it was
"recaptured" and "reappropriated" when it reappeared in Turkish architectural discourse in
a totally different context.

For Abdullah Ziya, the architectural strangeness of the carved dwelling lay
in its invisibility and its inability to be mapped. Unlike all the other village types that he
represented by architectural means (that is, plans and perspective drawings), the carved
dwellings could not be objectified. The task, then, was to render the latter visible. To
reenter architectural discourse, the carved dwelling had to acquire the three-dimensional
status of an architectural object. Not surprisingly, perhaps, one of the early attempts at its
proper representation is an axonometric projection that transformed carved spaces to the
orthogonal framework of wall-slab construction (fig. 4). The drawing shows a settlement in
Cappadocia, a central Anatolian region that is as well-known today by archeologists, art
historians, and architects as by casual tourists. As a matter of fact, Cappadocia had
captured the interest of Byzantinists since the end of the nineteenth century. Research
remained scattered, however, and mostly confined to art historical studies of the remains of
mosaics and paintings on the walls of a series of carved churches. A wave of "architectural"
interests invaded the Cappadocian carved dwellings only during the 1960s and 1970s.

An article by Suha Özkan and Selahattin Önür entitled "Another Thick Wall
Pattern" captures the nature of the new interest.[11] The title was derived from Christopher
Alexander's notion of "thick wall pattern," which emphasized flexibility in design based on
use. Cappadocian carved dwellings, according to the authors, had exploited that attribute
"for over fifteen hundred years." Other internationally acclaimed examples, such as David
Greene's Spray Plastic House and Paolo Soleri's Arcology project were also used in the
article in an attempt to include the Cappadocian carved dwelling in an international
category of similar forms. The authors argued that the Spray Plastic House was an example
of a carved house cut from a foam plastic block; it demonstrated a process "known to be
practiced in earth's formations over various parts of the world which are treated, more or

 10. Helene Cixous, *The Newly Born Woman* (Minneapolis: University of Minnesota Press, 1986), 71.
11. Suha Özkan and Selahattin Önür, "Another Thick Wall Pattern," in *Shelter, Sign and Symbol*, ed.
Paul Oliver (London: Barrie and Jenkins, 1975), 95–106.

less, like what one could call naturally available spaceframes. The Cappadocia region of Turkey is just one of them."[12] The Cappadocian carved settlements, according to the article, also satisfied the ecological concerns of Soleri's Arcology project. "Another Thick Wall Pattern" called the carved dwellings of Cappadocia to the attention of an international architectural audience for seemingly ahistorical qualities of flexibility and ecological and technological propriety. From this viewpoint, they could be comfortably placed in the same category with other structures, from other times and other places, that architectural discourse had already legitimized.

 A somewhat different logic of sameness operates in Paul Oliver's *Dwellings*, which covers housing traditions from a very broad geographical spectrum.[13] The section entitled "Carving a Home" focuses on a series of carved dwellings from the banks of the Yangtze river to Cappadocia and Southern Spain. Describing the Cappadocian landscape as "a Flemish master's dream of mountains," the author mostly concentrates on the building process. The essay flows effortlessly from one culture to the next, sometimes within the same paragraph. In the introduction to the book, Oliver asserts the intentional nature of this fluidity that is prevalent throughout the work:

> I wish to draw attention to the living and recent traditions. Almost inevitably, these have been largely in what are unsatisfactorily termed "The Third World," the "Developing World," or "Less Developed Countries," labels which are by no means easily defined and which are, in one way or another, divisive. As far as possible I have avoided using them, not wishing to make so arbitrary a distinction between nations, when my main emphasis is on cultures. Considering cultures has meant that within any one chapter, I have had to draw my examples from various parts of the globe.[14]

Specific types of building technologies, construction methods, and housing conditions form the basis of the comparative cultural study that follows.

 There are obvious differences between the arguments in "Another Thick Wall Pattern" and *Dwellings*. The former attempts to redefine the Cappadocian carved dwellings in terms of the most current architectural approaches. The latter is interested in their "vernacular" attributes of topographical, climatic, and cultural propriety, which prevail in traditional carved dwellings elsewhere. I would argue that the former's attempts to claim

12. Ibid., 96.
13. Paul Oliver, *Dwellings: The House Across the World* (Austin: University of Texas Press, 1987), 72.
14. Ibid., 11.

contemporaneity to the Cappadocian carved dwelling as opposed to the latter's regionalistic intentions are rooted in the differences between their sites of enunciation.

"Another Thick Wall Pattern" expresses the desire to legitimate a relatively unknown indigenous building type as a proper architectural category in international discourse. In that respect, it marks an ingenious convergence of two architectural fascinations of the 1960s: the (re)discovery of the "vernacular" and the utopian liberative promises of technology. Yet there is also the possibility of reading "Another Thick Wall Pattern" from another historiographical site. Similar architectural connections between local and Western traditions were made as early as the founding years of the Turkish republic, when regionalism was closely allied with nationalism. At that time, Sedad H. Eldem, a leading architectural figure who worked on traditional Turkish house types, made the bold statement that the characteristics of Turkish houses had been embodied in the residential works and architectural principles of modern masters like Frank Lloyd Wright and Le Corbusier.[15] Others related Turkish culture and lifestyles to such international modernist criteria as comfort, hygiene, and flexibility. The implication was that Turkish culture had always embodied the qualities that Western civilization had only recently discovered. All these were attempts to transcend the East/West, traditional/modern, natural/cultural oppositions to equalize differences in the interest of (inter)nationalist agendas. In so doing, they reinstated, rather than challenged, the terms by which the architectural discipline had been defined by Western masters.

The mission of *Dwellings*, on the other hand, is to expand the horizons of (Western) architectural/cultural knowledge; such a benevolent aim is prevalent in much of "vernacular studies." This mission is stated most explicitly in the introduction, "We need to know much more about these qualities that shape the dwelling of differing societies," the author suggests. "By doing so *we* may be more effective in assisting *them* in gaining appropriate living conditions—and in the process, learn more about *our own*."[16] *Dwellings* clearly perpetuates the binary logic of us/them that objectifies and appropriates the other in the interest of the self. It is typically located in the liberal framework of multiculturalism and cultural exchange that does not question the ambivalence of cultural authority.

I would argue that "Another Thick Wall Pattern" and *Dwellings*, in spite of their important differences, share a common basis that allows them to transform cultural

15. Sedad H. Eldem was involved in extensive documentation of traditional Turkish houses during the late 1920s and 1930s. See, "Elli Yillik Cumhuriyet Mimarliği" (Fifty Years of the Architecture of the Republic), *Mimarlik* 11 (1973): 6.
16. Oliver, *Dwellings*, 15, emphasis mine.

spaces into ahistorical cultural models of space despite, and because of, their best humanistic intentions. In Homi Bhabha's terms, they operate on the premises of "cultural diversity" rather than "cultural difference."[17] In both cases, such seemingly neutral concepts as user orientation, ecological soundness, and appropriate construction form the basis for the constitution of a family of theories/objects independent of both their location and the differences between the bodies/subjectivities that inhabit them.

Third Scene: Interruption

The first two instances that I have narrated in the long history of carved dwellings in Turkey mark significant moments of repression and assimilation. They reveal mechanisms by which architecture reinforces its boundaries in particular historical contexts in the constitution of its others. If the carved dwelling is named as the other of the conventional house, then the first two episodes exemplify the "settling down of the other" into the domain of the disciplinary boundaries of architecture.[18] The third one, on the other hand, marks a brief yet powerful moment of negotiation: it opens up a space that intervenes between proper architectural discourse and its objects of analysis. The recognition of this space challenges not only pre-given architectural categories but also the largely unproblematized premises of comparative multicultural analyses.

In my first two episodes, the carved dwellings in question were located in rural settings at a relatively safe distance from the learned architects' urban existence. As a matter of fact, professional architects went out to find, to name, and to silence them in the interest of their disciplinary framework.

My third episode takes place not in the countryside, but at the symbolic center of modern Turkey: the capital city of Ankara. This locational difference has considerable cultural and architectural implications. The spatial and temporal distance that separated urban architects from the rural settings in the first two scenes reinforced the unequal power relation involved in the construction of the binary opposites of urban/rural and modern/traditional. The vacated space between the architect and his cultural object, what I would call the place of lived spatiality, was not attended to, and was not powerful enough to interrupt the architect's one-way discourse. In other words, in the first two scenes the carved dwelling remained the mute object of architectural discourse. A strictly

17. Homi Bhabha states, "Cultural diversity is an epistemological object—culture as an object of empirical knowledge—whereas cultural difference is the process of the *enunciation* of culture as 'knowledge*able*' authoritative, adequate to the construction of systems of cultural identification. If cultural diversity is a category of comparative ethics, aesthetics or ethnology, cultural difference is a process of signification through which statements *of* culture or *on* culture differentiate, discriminate, and authorize the production of fields of force, reference, applicability, and capacity." Homi Bhabha, "The Commitment to Theory," in *The Location of Culture* (New York: Routledge, 1994), 34.
18. I borrowed this phrase from Helene Cixous. In *The Newly Born Woman* she asks, "What is the Other?" and explains, "If it is truly the 'other' there is nothing to say; it cannot be theorized. The 'other' escapes me. It is elsewhere, outside; absolutely other. It doesn't settle down. But in History, of

disciplinary discourse silenced other possible spatial narratives generated by its object of analysis. As Homi Bhabha observes in the context of contemporary criticism,

> The Other text is forever the exegetical horizon of difference, never the active agent of articulation. The Other is cited, quoted, framed, illuminated, encased in the shot/reverse shot strategy of a serial enlightenment.... The Other loses its power to signify, to negate, to initiate its historic desire, to establish its own institutional and oppositional discourse.[19]

I will argue that the brief appearance of the carved dwelling in the urban context of Ankara marks an interruption in the flow of proper architectural discourse, which has "cited, quoted, framed, [and] illuminated" it in the former two instances. The third instance marks a moment of negotiation and resistance where the carved dwelling enables the possibility of an oppositional discourse.

The site of my third scene is introduced in a 1949 newspaper report on squatter settlements in Ankara. The author, Adviye Fenik, narrates the following episode:

> Now we are on a secondary road. A street that is partially paved... I don't see dirt or garbage on the way... Only an upside-down earthen pot on the flattened roadside... I go to look. "Move back" say my friends, "you are on a roof." I am shocked; I shiver. How can there be people who live and dwell under the ground that I am stepping on? I walk backwards in grief as if I have crushed a tomb.... I see many upside down pots on my right, on my left, further away, and nearby.[20]

Fenik finds out that underground dwellings have been carved into the sloping ground between two roads leading to a hilltop. The upside-down earthen pots with holes at their bottom "function as chimneys as well as windows." "These are the most affordable squatters," she is told, "there is no need to worry about roofs and walls."

Squatter settlements were relatively new to Ankara when Fenik visited them in the late 1940s. Planned from scratch following the foundation of the Republic in 1923, Ankara was envisioned to be the symbol of enlightened modernity: clean, orderly, hygienic, and totally under the planners' control.[21] The mushrooming of squatter areas during numerous waves of rural migration beginning in the late 1930s, therefore, was most

course, what is called 'other' is an alterity that does settle down, that falls into the dialectical circle. It is the other in a hierarchically organized relationship in which the same is what rules, names, defines, and assigns 'its' other." Cixous, *Newly Born Woman*, 71.

19. Bhabha, "Commitment to Theory," 31.

20. Adviye Fenik, "Altindağ Röportajlari" (Altindağ Interviews), *Zafer*, 19 May 1949.

21. For an extensive analysis of the development of Ankara, see *Tarih İçinde Ankara* (Ankara in History), ed. Erdal Yavuz (Ankara: Middle East Technical University, 1980).

5
View from a squatter area in Ankara, 1949

6
Illustration from the front page of a 1937 newspaper

unwelcome by the city fathers (fig. 5). At that time the Minister of Interior Affairs assured the "citizens" that Ankara would be cleared from "these unsightly places with miserable roads."[22] Despite their reported cleanliness, squatter areas were usually described as "ugly" and "unsightly" and viewed as the city's garbage of which to be disposed. They rendered the city opaque by threatening the transparency of the newly built boulevards which had been proudly described as "the mirror of a beautiful and clean city" (fig. 6).[23] Yet the squatters furnished the very labor that made the boulevards possible. Their occupants—porters, maids, construction workers, taxi and bus drivers—were the very providers of the city's infrastructure. As Adviye Fenik recognized, "Wipe them off the map and the entire city will stop functioning as if there had been a power line cut."[24]

Not all squatter housing was carved dwellings, of course. In fact the latter's appearance was temporary as one of the tactical devices of the rural migrants to survive the city fathers' strategies to demolish their settlements. Other aspects of the physical environment of the squatter areas can also be read through these tactical operations. The mazelike sloping pathways, for example, that housed carved dwellings underneath and freestanding ones above enabled a kind of counter-control and surveillance for the inhabitants. The opacity of the maze enabled an entire neighborhood network of communication that was vocal and gestural rather than visual. By activating that network, the news of an intruder, usually the police who delivered the order for eviction, reached all the way to the summit within a matter of minutes.[25] Thus the carved dwellings provided an architectural answer to the threat of eviction. In addition, they were inexpensive to build, difficult to notice, and almost impossible to demolish.

From an architectural viewpoint, the carved dwellings of the squatter areas disrupt historical accounts that delegate them to a premodern past. Here they are the very products of the modern city. Despite reproducing the form of rural carved dwellings, they do not symbolize a primitive or prearchitectural existence. In other words, the carved dwellings of the squatter settlements neither fulfill architecture's urban aspirations nor its romanticized rural image. On one hand, they challenge the fixed polarities of traditional/modern and rural/urban. (Here they are both/neither traditional and/nor modern, both/neither rural and/nor urban.) On the other hand, they reveal the partial, precarious, and limited nature of architectural truths.

22. Tansi Şenyapili, *Ankara Kentinde Gecekondu Gelisimi: 1923–1960* (The Development of Squatters in Ankara: 1923–1960) (Ankara: Kent Koop Yay, 1985), 57–58.
23. The caption to this image read, "Asphalt road after rain. In the illustration above, you see the reflection of an Ankara scene on the asphalt road after last night's rain. In view of this, we can repeat the aphorism that an asphalt road is the mirror of a beautiful and clean city."
24. Adviye Fenik, "Altindağ Röportajlari" (Altindağ Interviews), *Zafer*, 13 May 1949 Among a large amount of statistical, economical, and administrative analyses of the early squatter settlements in Ankara, Fenik's newspaper series is the only account that I know of on everyday-life phenomena. Her report is invaluable in providing insight into the tactical operations of *gecekondu* environments. Architectural discourse and practice, on the other hand, which had been obsessed with rural

It is hardly surprising, therefore, that unlike the "negative villages" the carved dwellings of the squatters never came to the architects' attention. Since they produced new and hybrid articulations, these dwellings defy conventional architectural analyses at a number of levels. First of all, unlike most other buildings that are monumentalized by architectural discourse, they are not built on the premises of visibility and permanence. Squatter housing is under continuous threat of demolishment and is expandable depending on growing family size and income. Second, the primary concern of their builders is not climatic and topographical propriety. In carving their dwellings, rural migrants responded less to such criteria cherished by regionalists than to the very conditions that simultaneously affirmed and denied their urban existence.[26] The carved dwellings of the squatters are exemplary in showing that proper architectural discourse remains silent when it faces the complex network of relationships between subjectivity, power, and space.

Prospects

In my account of three different appearances of the carved dwelling in the building practice and architectural discourse of modern Turkey, I addressed specific issues concerning the limits of proper architectural discourse. Neither my choice of the carved dwelling as an architectural category nor the sequence of my narrative (naming, assimilation, and interruption) is meant to be conclusive; the issues that were raised, such as the narrative of origins, the colonization of the "vernacular," and the status of squatters in architectural discourse, range far beyond the particularities of the moments in question.

In the first two scenes, I emphasized specific architectural agendas centered around the reproducibility of the carved dwelling. Abdullah Ziya's research on rural Turkey clearly would have contributed to the modernist and nationalist discourses of the 1930s. His diagnoses would have helped transform the physical environment of rural Turkey based on modernist standards, while his architectural findings would have contributed to the foundation of a new Turkish architecture based on the country's folk traditions. In the case of the carved dwellings of the "negative villages," he recognized that there was nothing to reproduce, to reform, or to use. Hence there was no architecture—only bodies yet to be "properly" housed. The second scene, in its various manifestations, incorporated the carved

buildings and settings, remained silent about all these phenomena.

25. Nursun Ertuğrul, "Gecekondu Yapim Süreci: Akdere'den bir Örnek" (The Building of Squatter Houses: A Case Study in Akdere), *Mimarlik* 3 (1977): 105.

26. Squatter settlements still mushroom in Ankara and other major cities. Their status keeps changing, however, depending on shifting policies and city regulations, which are intricately interwoven with party politics. Such analysis is obviously outside the scope of this essay but is extensively covered in studies by Mübeccel Kiray and Tansi Şenyapili.

dwelling into the proper boundaries of architecture. The latter gained architectural status under the partial and selective gaze of the discipline. Finally, the appearance of the carved dwelling in the squatter areas of modern Ankara remains conspicuously absent from architectural discourse. I have attributed this absence to the challenge that it presented to the categorical boundaries of architectural knowledge. In this case the carved dwelling "spoke back" not only to architecture but also to the city and its disciplinary mechanisms by actively resisting their appropriative practices. The recognition of this phenomenon calls for explorations of similar instances of resistance and negotiation during the processes of naming and assimilation. I will narrate one such moment as a means of initiating such discourse although it does not have any direct bearing on architecture.

At the same time that Abdullah Ziya was categorizing rural Turkish settlements, another enlightened reformer, Nusret Köymen, was emphasizing some fundamental difficulties in pursuing the civilizing mission in rural Turkey. Most remarkably, Köymen pointed to the incommensurability between urban and rural cultural practices. "The languages of the urban dweller and the peasant are different even if they use the same words," he stated. "[They are different] to such extent that a peasant from a village who had no contact with any city and an urban dweller who had no previous rural exposure cannot possibly understand each other.... There is no way to cancel this difference."[27] In the city, he continued, since there was no possibility of communication, the peasants refused to speak. They "merely nodded" at whatever they heard. Unlike most of his contemporaries, Köymen recognized the gesture of nodding as the refusal to speak rather than as a sign of acceptance or agreement. His interruption of the silent act of nodding enabled him to recognize the rural other as a subject rather than a mere object of his analysis.

My exploration of the appearance of the carved dwelling in the urban scene is an attempt to capture such an instance of resistance and negotiation in a spatial/architectural context. These instances, however momentary they might be, force a recognition of complex cultural and spatial fabrics that challenges both architecture's focus on *a-priori* formal categories and its emphasis on comparative multicultural analysis. If the meaning and symbols of culture have no primordial unity or fixity, a focus on the processes of negotiation in the immediacy of spatial practices may provide openings to liberate the discipline of architecture from its binary closures.

27. Nusret Köymen, "Köyçülüğün Daha Verimli Olmasi Hakkinda Düşünceler (Thoughts on Increasing Productivity in Rural Reforms), *Ülkü*, vol. 13, no. 73 (March 1939): 27.

Abjection and Architecture:
The Migrant House in Multicultural Australia
Mirjana Lozanovska

Preamble

This preamble is a *meze*,[1] a taste of the state of multiculturalism in Australia and its popular reconstitution as a form of nationalism, which is reproduced via the dominant information apparatus—television. More specifically it is a taste of how a discourse of architectural monuments is entangled with the consumption of rice. My thesis is that multiculturalism is only digestible as food, but food is only digestible as "exotic tourism"; multiculturalism and architecture are doubly displaced.

Looking at figure 1, I am impressed with the fluid relationship between food and form as the moving image on the screen demonstrates that an ordinary bowl of rice can transform itself into a solid geometric cultural monument—Big Ben ("an old English rice pudding"), Manhattan ("Manhattan meat balls"), Taj Mahal ("an Indian curry"), and the Leaning Tower of Pisa ("an Italian risotto")—and back again into the ordinary steaming bowl of rice. The narration implicates an Australia that consumes food from many different cultures, "Most Versatile Rice. The Best Under the Australian Sun. Calrose Sunwhite." Leaving aside the instantaneousness of the transformation, I am more curious about two other effects of the moving image: the cultural significance of a transformation between food and monument within a "multicultural" Australia and the strangely mythic dimension as the images hang precariously between a gingerbread house and a deconstructionist building as an architecture that defies its necessity for a "ground." I had watched this advertisement many times before (around 11:00 P.M., channel 9, Tuesday nights), always seduced by the technological feat of making a bowl of rice into a solid monument. Is it glued? Is it boiled sticky rice? Is it polystyrene reproduced to look like rice? This pursuit to find the technological truth was only temporary; it lasted the length of the advertisement. I was just happy to be entertained in such a clever way. However one night, as I was watching the ad (and writing this article), I was struck in that piercing kind of way and my seduction started to take on a horrifying sort of turn; as it happens with abjection, my stomach turned.

---

1. *Meze* is a Macedonian ritual and word for hors d'oeuvres or antipasto, which are other untranslatable words and cultural practices.

1
Rice advertisement,
Calrose Sunwhite
Rice, Channel 9,
Melbourne

A thousand questions presented themselves, simple questions necessary for the postcolonial female theorist. What was I being fed—a humble dish of rice, a Third-World food in the form of a "postcard" monument? Which nimble fingers, migrant or Third World, worked these tiny grains into a sculpture (I was reminded of those single-grain carvings done by Chinese artists)? These monuments spanned the globe, producing a geographic planar equality, but what had this to do with multiculturalism in Australia? Why was the rice, and therefore the monuments, white? What sort of hegemonic, chromatic[2] nationalism was this advocating? What sort of attack was it on the "yellow" race that is perceived globally as the origin/consumer of "white" rice? How would have brown rice been appropriated by advertising, or by the different cultural/class groups?

How was I seduced? Monuments—architectural, sublime objects—implied a complicity between technology and aesthetics (governed by the primacy of visuality) and advertising (a major exponent of late-capitalist power apparati). I was fed image and form instead of food. Digestibility is dependent on formalism and formalism is dependent on tourism—multiculturalism and rice are only digestible if appropriated by a "postcard" aesthetic. This advertisement was definitely not only about eating rice. It was also about the visual consumption of nationalism, the consumption of an "All Australian Calrose White Rice." But more dangerous was the underlying primacy of "visuality" instituted against the possibility of a "speaking" multiculturalism, that is, against the most threatening productive dimension of the tongue—speaking. While making reference to the tasting tongue, the tongue that consumes, the commercial made no reference to the speaking tongue. Different languages and different words were silenced. Production of a speaking multiculturalism was disavowed from the start. The transformation from the food to the monument was a method by which the hegemonic culture constructed its own version of multiculturalism, not a heterogeneous and irreducible version that is in multiple play, but a glamorous postcard version that is homogenized and controlled in the perverse mode of technology controlling nimble fingers. The effect is that speaking about migration, multiculturalism, and ethnicity in ways that constitute cultural difference is disavowed, but that speaking is nonetheless threatening.

And whose desire is this? Out of the rice grains heaped in a bowl—formless food, signifier of a maternal-feminine—rise solid vertical monuments. The conversion of

2. See Spivak's use of this word. Gayatri Chakravorty Spivak, *The Post-Colonial Critic: Interviews, Strategies, Dialogues,* ed. Sarah Harasym (New York: Routledge, 1990), 62.

food into monument is a metaphor for the "original" metaphor-making, which is necessary to make the journey from the unintelligible formless space of the maternal into a symbolic form mediated by the phallus.

I will discuss the dual role that the migrant house and the migrant "enclave" as spatial zones play in deconstructing a persistent and mythic yet very problematic hegemonic culture in Australia and (de)constructing a (provisional) identity for the migrant. My argument is sited at the potent and unsettling zones between spatiality and theories of subjectivity that emphasize language. Language is established as that which constitutes the speaking social being, especially in the Lacanian schema in which human subjects come into being not so much by acquiring language as by their insertion into an already existing order of language and the law: the symbolic order.[3] Spatiality on the other hand is not something that is established within discursive practices in ways that articulate a horizon of meanings and effects, and yet it is used as an "assumed" term extensively in recent discussions across disciplines. There is much ambiguity and blurring of the boundaries around the issue of spatiality. If, for example, it is related to the space in and of the body, where is its limit? The body as a bounded and finite entity is a concept that has been thoroughly interrogated.[4] The idea that the subject is fixed and occupies a centralized position in space is no longer tenable—space no longer serves the subject in this way. The migrant house is a literal site in which an adult is inserted into a preexisting order of language. This raises some significant questions about the spatial relations by which different subjectivities are produced. The undiscussed relationship between spatiality and subjectivity and its specific effects on the existing order of language is explored in this essay. Spatiality is not inert, passive, or merely "mental space" that can be (linguistically) codified and decodified; nor is it merely "opaque space" that can be measured empirically.[5] The speculative aspect of my argument is that there is more to space and spatiality than a linguistic appropriation, and therefore there is more to the relations between spatiality and language in the construction of the subject as a social, speaking being and as a spatially embodied being.

Migration

The city is a significant vision for the becoming of a male migrant. Late-capitalist forces structure his desires for the city differently than those of the bourgeois

3. For an explanation of subjectivity and the symbolic order, see Elizabeth Grosz, *Sexual Subversions: Three French Feminists* (Sydney: Allen and Unwin, 1989) and Jane Gallop, *Reading Lacan* (Ithaca, NY: Cornell University Press, 1985).
4. Some theorists who have been concerned with the concept of the body across many of their texts include Michel Foucault, Moira Gatens, Elizabeth Grosz, and Luce Irigaray.
5. Henri Lefebvre points to the inadequacies of the dominant reductive theorizations of space: space as either "mental" space or "opaque" space. Henri Lefebvre, *The Production of Space*, trans. D. Nicholson-Smith (Oxford: Blackwell, 1991). Irigaray's essay on "The 'Mechanics' of Fluids," is an incisive account of the complicit relations between rationality, form, and a mechanics of solids. In this economy "woman" serves as a "geometric prop" and/or excessive "congealed interval;" fluidity and

subject of the First World and differently than those of a female migrant. In *A Seventh Man* John Berger and Jean Mohr's descriptions suggest the layerings of the image of the city and the spoken word:

> Everyday he hears about the metropolis. The name of the city changes. It is all cities, overlaying one another and becoming a city that exists nowhere but which continually transmits promises. . . . Envisaged, the future about to begin is a wall, not a space: a wall not unlike the wall of an ancient city, except that its surface is not time-honored and hand-cut but time-defying and like the surface of a television screen behind which random images appear, yet which, when empty, is an opaque cloud that nothing can penetrate.[6]

These descriptions suggest the structuration of the drive to leave, to become a migrant. Notions of Utopia (the ideal city and the dream house, the ideal/dream) are constructed through stories, through fabrications by those that return, through a strange mixture between the experience of a journey in space and its narration in language. Cities are reinterpreted, translated, and sublimated in the language of the migrant. The distinction between a wall and a space is a significant site for the exploration of the relation between architecture and subjectivity. Berger and Mohr's distinction suggests that the historical construct of a "wall" as a physical configuration is transformed into something that is mediated by technology into a screen, which is equally impenetrable. My study does not tackle technology as such; rather, it illustrates that at the very site of the "wall" as an architectural configuration, at the very "wall" constructed by the migrant, the issue of (im)penetration is at the least not stable. At the very site that is intended as a frontier, the wall produces a convolution in and of space. Space is turned inside-out. External walls constitute an architectural excess, an aesthetic-psychic effect, in which "fixed" subjects turn in on themselves and others produce temporary provisional limits.

Gayatri Chakravorty Spivak's statement "to ignore the subaltern today is, willy-nilly, to continue the imperialist project" is a direct critique of the negation of representational processes within some poststructuralist positions.[7] In writing about the migrant in multicultural Australia these parameters of the European sovereign subject and the subaltern are differently constructed. Australia has a complicated relation to contemporary postcolonial studies. Its historical narratives as a colony of the British empire

104   her becoming are impossible. Luce Irigaray, *This Sex Which Is Not One*, trans. C. Porter and C. Burke (Ithaca, NY: Cornell University Press, 1985), 108.

6. John Berger and Jean Mohr, *A Seventh Man: The Story of a Migrant Worker in Europe* (Cambridge: Granta Books and Penguin Books, 1989), 23, 60.

7. Gayatri Chakravorty Spivak, "Can the Subaltern Speak?," *Marxism and the Interpretation of Culture*, ed. C. Nelson and L. Grossberg (Chicago: University of Illinois Press, 1988), 298. This book is a critique against the claim that "the oppressed can speak for themselves." Spivak argues that a First-World intellectual masquerading as absent non-representor may disguise in this transparency a complicity with the investigating subject, and thus reconstitute the mechanics of the colonizer. Her critique is specifically of Michel Foucault and Gilles Deleuze.

and as an industrially advanced nation that has put into practice extensive migration policies have conflictual and contradictory effects. The institutional discourse of Australia is monolingual, unlike that of Canada, for example, which is bilingual. On this and many levels Australia's reference is specifically the United Kingdom. A division between England and Europe as the origin for culture is in effect in Australia. To say you are a "laboring migrant"[8] from Europe, "a European," is to identify with a marginal group. The hegemonic culture in Australia, through a complex network of forces (America is thrown in there too), is mediated firstly by England, and only at a second level of colonization by Europe. Southern European migrants[9] coming from the lower working or peasant classes are particular subalterns within the diaspora of Australia, and it is their specific stereotyping that I will disclose and disrupt in this paper.

The White Australian Policy, a policy that monitored non-British immigration to Australia, governed the entire period between federation in 1901 and the Whitlam government in 1972. It established a program to select people for their particular capacity to assimilate and to assure the Australian population that the migrants would only fill gaps in the economic system that they (the real Australians) did not want. It was explicitly a racially exclusionist policy, specifically aimed against Asian migrants.[10] It aimed for total assimilation. Of the potential European migrants it differentiated between northern and southern Europeans, with preferences for Nordic, Aryan types; the southern Europeans were considered less racially desirable.[11] These policies enforced a construction of Australia as a nation with clearly established British origins and a unified cultural frontier of an Anglo-Celtic combination.[12] As one historical text points out, the paradox of Australia's extensive immigration policies, policies that produced one of the world's most ethnically diverse countries, is that it did so by advocating the superiority of British culture.[13] Only once the northern European sources (middle-class refugees) were no longer available (due to economic growth in those countries) did Australia introduce policies that targeted "unskilled" migrants from southern Europe. While these migrants were not actually "unskilled" this label enabled them to be used as factory laborers, as well as to be seen as a homogenized group from a peasant background. They arrived in the postwar period of the 1950s; by the mid 1960s, when the Australian economy once again improved and targeted a wider geographic pool of potential migrants, the place of the

8. This is an awkward term to describe migrants that are "invited" into the country for their capacity to labor, i.e., manual work.

9. Specifically the migrant from Macedonia.

10. For further analysis of these policies in respect to Asians, see, Stephen Castle, et al., eds., *Mistaken Identity: Multiculturalism and the Demise of Nationalism in Australia*, 2nd edition (Sydney: Pluto Press, 1988), chapter 3, "Assimilation to Integration 1972–1987" and chapter 4, "The Construction of Ethnicity 1972–1987."

11. See Srebrenka Kunek, "Brides, Wives and Single Women: Gender and Immigration," *Lilith: A Feminist History Journal* 8 (Summer 1993): 82–113.

12. See Sneja Gunew, "Home and Away: Nostalgia in Australian (Migrant) Writing," in *Island in the*

migrant was already outlined, "the introduction of the migrant worker at the bottom of the ladder often meant promotion or upgrading for Australian workers and relieved them of the necessity to seek employment in remote areas of an arduous character."[14]

Migrant culture has not been assimilated into Australian culture. Instead, "British"-derived culture continues to structure Australian institutions, professional networks, and national identity to the present day. To ignore the "subaltern/migrant"[15] continues the imperialist project, to not ignore the subaltern entails its own problems about theorizing difference and ethnicity. The problem of representation is taken up in a conversation between Gayatri Chakravorty Spivak and Sneja Gunew, two leading theorists of culture:

> SG: I think that one forgets when one speaks within very obviously privi-leged academic contexts about, say, immigrant groups within Australia, that one is very much in danger of homogenizing, and of misrepresenting. . . .
>
> GCS: I don't think, really, that we will solve the problem today. . . I think it has to be kept alive as a problem. It is not a solution, the idea of the disenfranchised speaking for themselves.[16]

The migrant house as an object of study is marginalized in at least two disciplines. In cultural and literary studies the margins are constructed by being labeled as other than the main. As Gunew explains, terms such as "migrant writing" suggest that the only acceptable subaltern speaking position is a homogeneous, "authentic" migrant voice. In architectural discourses the migrant house has not even entered as a tokenistic measure. The only legitimate "migrant house" to discuss might be an individual house designed by a non-migrant architect. Individualism in this sense is overdetermined by ethnicity, class, and gender. The migrant house that is the focus of this paper is the house built by first-generation migrants of southern European descent who migrated in the 1960s. My task here is to explore the stereotypical in a way that opens possibilities for an eruption of the other. The houses were generally built in the mid 1970s to early 1980s, in the period when the "migrants" had moved into the "lower middle working classes" in an economic sense, given that the notion of "class" is problematic when culture and ethnicity also structure status and identity. If the intention in the initial postwar policies was to have migrants fill gaps rather than contest space, the construction of these houses and "enclaves" constitutes

106   *Stream*, ed. P. Foss (Sydney: Pluto Press, 1988).

13. See Castles, *Mistaken Identity*, 50.

14. Arthur Monk, secretary of the Australian Council of Trade Unions, cited in ibid., 54.

15. While I am borrowing from Spivak's paper, "Can the Subaltern Speak," clearly there are distinctions between her deployments of the term "subaltern" and the term "migrant." For one the migrant is not a colonized person, and in this strict sense only an Aboriginal may be considered a "subaltern." But I do not think that the term subaltern is necessarily so strict; for example, it may be an apt term for migrants from India, after colonization. In its general sense it is a term for a marginal group who do not have the privilege for self-representation. Thus while there are distinctions between "subaltern" and "migrant" there are also profound overlaps.

some sort of territorial claim that not only contests such an intention but that is a constant threat to Australia's difficulty, as a nation, to deal with cultural difference.

The title of this paper comprises two incongruous and problematic terms, "migrant" and "multicultural." It is important to note that while the status as "migrant" is officially temporary, its endurance as a label is a way of perpetuating the host/guest inequality of residents in Australia. Gunew distinguishes between two types of multiculturalism: "a system of government policies designed to manage cultural diversity, and multiculturalism insofar as it arises from the desires of various communities and individuals who feel excluded by the discourses and practices surrounding Australian nationalism."[17] In the policy definition, multiculturalism is advocated as "cultural diversity," which serves to eclipse both unequal power relations and the challenge to a homogeneous national culture. Histories of migration and histories of multiculturalism are not the same; continuing attempts to conflate the two are ways of reducing the social condition of multiculturalism to a temporary status, implying that the real desire is to move "beyond" multiculturalism. My title is a play on binary divisions—temporary/permanent, migrant/resident, migration/multiculturalism—as an initial proliferation of difference. My own position in relation to the marginalization of the migrant house within both cultural and architectural disciplines is captured by Spivak's reply to Gunew's question about the way in which the "authentic" migrant voice comes back to us constructed by hegemonic voices:

> Subordinate people use this also; and we are not without a sense of irony: we use it. I talk a lot, right? And when I get very excited I interrupt people; and I am making a joke, but in fact it is never perceived as a joke unless I tell them. I will quite often say, "You know, in my culture it shows interest and respect if someone interrupts": and immediately there are these very pious faces, and people allow me to interrupt. It is not as if we don't perceive the homogenization; we exploit it, why not?[18]

This paper is just that—an interruption, an interruption in the academic discourses about a stereotypical image of a migrant house. This response is a gesture of my "ethnic" position in relation to feminism as it is constituted within Australian institutions and culture, as well as in relation to the "nationalizing" discourses in cultural studies and the "universalizing" discourses in architecture.

107   16. Sneja Gunew and Gayatri Chakravorty Spivak, "Questions of Multiculturalism," in Spivak, *Post-Colonial Critic*, 63.
17. Sneja Gunew, "Feminism and the Politics of Irreducible Differences: Multi-culturalism/ethnicity/race," in *Feminism and the Politics of Difference*, ed. Sneja Gunew & Anna Yeatman (Sydney: Allen & Unwin, 1993), 2.
18. Spivak, *Post-Colonial Critic*, 61.

Pečalbari Pustina

Eagles and lions are mythical and masculine symbols of war and defense. The hegemonic culture in Australia recognizes migrant houses by these mythical creatures that guard the gateways and sometimes the site perimeter of the migrant territory (figs. 2 and 3). The migrant houses are perceived as big and labeled "Mediterranean Palaces" by the hegemonic culture, although in actuality they are not half as big as the houses built by the elite on the other side of the river.[19] Eagles and lions adorn the gateways of the big migrant houses in a masculine gesture to fend off the enemy. But who is this enemy? What is being protected? What drives this extreme division between interior and exterior—this "wall of war" architecture?

Migration is a movement across geographical boundaries but it is also a movement from one symbolic order, one paternal language and law, to another.[20] A better spatial metaphor than moving across a map might be falling off the map, a journey in which the migrant is left with an empty space where that other imaginary identity might have been:

> We were so big there and could do everything. When you have lots you know it. Lucky and lucky and money. My father was the tallest man in the world. Here we were nothing. There vet in the district and respect. The head of the returned soldiers and medals. Here washed floors in the serum laboratory. Shrinking man. I grow smaller everyday. The world gets too big for me. We were too small for this big country.[21]

Maps historically have been tools for the establishment of a place.[22] While maps are constituted through technics of space, these intersect with strategies of language; Hoddle, King, William, Queen, and Elizabeth streets in Melbourne reference the cultural and historical "origins" of Melbourne. Melbourne is a city that is recognized for its relentless "grid," it is as though a net were simply thrown over the land, but the lines of this net are named, and these names establish English as the language of a preexisting symbolic order into which the migrant is inserted. Maps are territorializations of space through layered forces of language as well as technics of space.

Marginalized groups are not likely to mistake themselves for the "universal man"; migrants have the sense that they are "fragmented" or not "fixed."[23] Men are emascu-

19. Melbourne is divided in a geographical and mythical tracing by the Yarra River. East and south of the river is thought of as elite, both established and entrepreneurial; north and west is reproduced as the "labor heartland."

20. In another sense the original symbolic order was already made into a condition of marginality; Berger and Mohr explain it as a process of being made underdeveloped. It may be that in the process of de-centering, Europe sacrificed and made into the "other" its own blurred edges—the Mediterranean, the Eastern Block, and the Balkans. The more recent re-centering processes of the European Community are redrawing the borders once again.

21. Ania Walwicz, cited in Sneja Gunew, "Beyond the Echo: Migrant Writing and Australian Literature," in *Displaced Persons*, ed. Kirsten Holst Petersen and Anna Rutherford (Sydney: Dangaroo Press, 1988).

lated; in John Berger and Jean Mohr's *A Seventh Man*, the male migrant's body is subjected to a scientific gaze and produced within a global economy of technological development and underdevelopment.[24] He exchanges his body for the chance of economic existence; it is a gamble. His loss of the "phallus" is signified in the gaze at his penis by a woman in a white laboratory coat. Crossing geographic boundaries involves cross-dressings of gender: women are dressed as men and migrant men are undressed, their masculinity disclosed.

A line inscribed onto the global map connects the old country and the new country. The world is already mapped by and through the Cartesian net that constructs spatiality as a geometric veil. The line of the migrant's journey is a graphic superimposition onto this veil. It denies the temporal journey that migration as movement entails, and yet it is a remainder of the migrant's utopian gesture—to migrate, to go to the city. But the line is also a scar on the uniformity of the global net. It is sewn up, it is a trace of a split, a cut. In the line between the language of the symbolic order that one enters and the old language, the symbolic power of the phallus is diminished, sewn over as though it were a wound. The migrant is a decentered subject; migration has triggered a break from the illusory unity of the self. The story of the other has already begun. Every story is a travel story, but the story of migration is a particular surfacing of the foreigner within ourselves. Such a migrational movement is specifically from an "elsewhere," somewhere not on the global map, to the city, to the ideal city, the city with a name.

The split subject is multilayered in terms of class, gender, ethnicity, and race. My task here is to explore the impossible recovery of the migrant woman through an exploration of architectural space. The migrant as woman is frequently blocked by narratives of the migrant as man, as much as it is kept mute behind the screen of Western feminist theoretical agendas. To Spivak's question, "Can the Subaltern Speak?," my response is indirect, obtuse perhaps, and shifts the emphasis from boundaries of languages to boundaries of architecture, to physical walls. What are the relations between these boundaries, between architectural frontiers and the surfacing of unspoken words? In what ways do conditions of spatiality within the migrant house produce possibilities for the becoming of (female) migrant subjectivities? The architecture of the migrant house produces frontiers and spatial conditions for an eruption of a decentered subjectivity that both dismantles hegemonic hierarchies and breaks out in a poetics/politics of difference:

22. See Michel de Certeau, *The Practice of Everyday Life*, trans. S. F. Rendall (Berkeley: University of California Press, 1984).

23. See Sneja Gunew, "PMT (Post Modernist Tensions): Reading for (Multi)Cultural Difference," in *Striking Chords: Multicultural Literary Interpretations* (Sydney: Allen & Unwin, 1992), 45.

24. Berger and Mohr, *Seventh Man*, 45–52.

Such a poetics would conceive the self not as the product of its different identity from others but as constructed by multiple differences within and from itself. . . . It is a complex, multiple, layered subject with agency in the discourses and the worlds that constitute the referential space of his or her autobiography.[25]

To claim that the migrant house is a site of the abject is to interpret architecture as a force that transgresses cultural frontiers. The migrant house signifies the abject culturally, in relation to a hegemonic culture, and individually, in relation to the migrant identity. These two moments of the abject are nested one within the other in a mode like that of Roland Barthes's diagrammatic analysis of myths.[26] For Barthes the signifier is both the final term of the linguistic system and the first term of the mythical system; it is the point of a sideways shift, a movement across linguistic structures.

This can be illustrated by the lions and eagles that are constructed as the gateway keepers of the migrant frontier. Architecturally the surface articulation or point of contact between the two levels of the abject is figured by the lions and the eagles on the site perimeter. But this point is the point of transfer from object to abject—the gatekeepers are no longer just ornamental objects. They are a sign of the migrant house as not merely an object, but a mythic symbol of cultural terrorism. At the point at which they are constructed as the myth about migrants, their objectivity produces an effect best described by the spatial metaphor "to turn inside out," a spatial/psychic effect. Architectural objects— the lions and the eagles—transgress their own objective boundaries and enter the field of mythic and psychic signifiers. Through an effect of architectural objectification, structures are destabilized rather than established.

What do these figures signify for the migrant, and what do they signify for the hegemonic culture? As visible objects, do they transfer signification between individual and culture? For the migrant these figures are images of power and force, images of territorializations, of a frontier in and of space. Yet in their transfer into the suburban environment they become targets for the common gesture of finger pointing—a gesture of military intent in the cultural battlefield. The eagles and lions are reduced in size by this act. Thus, in the transfer into mythic signification they become figures of the marginal;

25. Shirley Neuman, cited in Gunew, "Feminism and Politics," 11.
26. See Roland Barthes, *Mythologies*, trans. A. Lavers (London: Paladin Grafton Books, 1972), 115. Barthes describes myth as "a second-order semiological system" constructed from a semiological chain that existed before it. Myth is a second language, in which one speaks about the first.

they signify the migrant as noncitizen, as other. These territorial gestures are rendered into the migrant's incapacity to assimilate.

What sort of suburban environment is implicated by the necessity for symbolic gatekeepers? As figures of war and defense they signify that the environment is a hostile territory. They make visible mythic territorial divisions. Distinct territorial claims surface in the "normalized" suburban environment. There is indeed much confusion: can these figures that are signifiers of cultural abjection for the hegemonic culture also be a defensive gesture about territory for the migrant? They become figures of resistance, of strategy in a context of military maneuvers. But the hegemonic culture disclaims the possibility of war—from its point of view there is no other side, there is no other. It is the very construction of an architectural frontier that has confronted the hegemonic culture with the other. The lions and eagles become the sign for the abject; that is, they are no longer objects within a subject/object bifurcation. They signify that the host/guest structure no longer holds. The abject though is also the limit to games of war because it is a condition without the possibility of strategic positions. It alters the structure of interaction from visibility and pointing (panoptic missiles) to utterances, exclamations, and, as we shall see, babble and oral disgust.

In looking at the migrant house it has been necessary to look at how the condition of the abject is articulated in psychoanalytic theories and in theories of culture. My point of departure is the work of Julia Kristeva on abjection, and Mary Douglas on "purity and danger," specifically interpreted to explore the layered levels of the abject that operate through the bodies of the migrant and host around the migrant house. The migrant house is the site in which the conditions of the abject are seen to mediate between the individual psychic being (Kristeva) and the production of culture (Douglas). Kristeva's work on personal revulsion and Douglas's work on social taboos explore the varying degrees of horror and fear in the response to those unidentifiable "matters" that transgress borders and boundaries, bodily fluids: feces, spit, sperm, tears, menstrual blood, breast milk, urine, vomit, mucus, saliva, and sexual fluids.[27] Douglas constructs the body as a bounded system; she argues that the monitoring of its bodily orifices emphasizes the "danger" of the ambiguous matter that passes through in the same way that the monitoring of architectural exits and entries emphasizes the threat of social disorder, constituted as a

27. See Julia Kristeva, *Powers of Horror: An Essay on Abjection*, trans. L. S. Roudiez (New York: Columbia University Press, 1982) and Mary Douglas, *Purity and Danger: An Analysis of Concepts of Pollution and Taboo* (Harmondsworth, UK: Pelican Books, 1966).

spatial confusion and a spatial ambiguity. Kristeva's work focuses on the body as a necessary precondition for subjectivity. The very inability to either identify these fluids, products, and traces as part of the body (and therefore constitute the subject) or completely separate and distinct from the body (as objects) articulates in part the condition of abjection. The abject is a preoedipal phase that is identified with the feminine and the maternal as a precondition for a self-contained and autonomous speaking social subject, a subject associated with the paternal and the phallus-governed symbolic order.[28] Thus, a "'proper' subjectivity and sociality are founded on the (impossible) expulsion or exclusion of the improper, the unclean, and the disorderly."[29] Put simply, abjection is a confusion of the division between subject and object that functions around the configuration of the body. What abjection puts at stake, according to Kristeva's profound analysis, is the subject itself. But which subject?

My argument is twofold. Firstly migrants are seen, as having to negotiate a new symbolic in the psychoanalytic sense so that their old languages (within the law of the father) are repressed, or become constructed as the abject in the Kristevan sense. To create a clean and proper language, they need to suppress and expel their previous language, so that not only the mother but the mother tongue is denied.[30]

The migrant house is one site in which these processes of negotiation occur, processes that involve the task of keeping the abject at bay.

Secondly, while the "citizen" subject dismisses the migrant house, the migrant house triggers a response in which the hegemonic culture is caught in a space of the abject. The subject is in perpetual danger of abjection signified by the migrant house. The image of the migrant houses, symbolically ignored while physically present on the borders of the architectural and urban environment, represents the claim of both Douglas and Kristeva that what is negated and repressed can never be totally removed.

Kyká Majka

Through the metaphoric and metonymic inscriptions of the mother(land) onto the architecture of the house, the migrant house as a space of the abject becomes a precarious sort of "projection." The architectural projections of "big" houses are both

28. Elizabeth Grosz states that the semiotic, the maternal *chora* and the abject are all placed on the side of the feminine and the maternal, which is a very complicated zone of psychoanalytic theory, in Grosz, *Sexual Subversions*, 78.

29. Elizabeth Grosz, "Language and the Limits of the Body: Kristeva and Abjection," in *Futur*Fall: Excursions into Post-Modernity*, ed. Elizabeth Grosz et al. (Sydney: Pathfinder Press and Power Institute, 1987), 108.

30. Gunew, "Feminism and Politics," 14.

sustained and maintained by the migrants while at the same time enclosing them. "Big" houses are territorial claims that are spatially excessive in various ways—in scale, in the duration of the materials (concrete, bricks), in security marked by the fence and doors, in ornament (lions and eagles), and in the extreme properness marked by the control of "nature." The "big" houses might be seen as metaphoric substitutes for the loss of the motherland. For the migrant (man and woman) "mother" is an architectural concept, the mother's body is the house. Yet this house is not able to be objectified; rather, it creates a space in which an ambiguous relationship is formed between the migrant's body and the architecture of the house. The migrant's body, a body whose limits are marked by its non-representation within the hegemonic culture, is marked by a lack that renders it a fatigued body, a sick body, a body in need. The house is presented as the clean and proper body in which architectural order prevails—gateway, symmetry, front entry, facade. The house gets bigger. It is marked by various architectural excesses while its occupant's body diminishes.

The house as a mother figures frequently in narrative as the psychosexual space of the repressed in the masculine subject.[31] It is represented as the architecture of a male fantasy, a signification of protection for the male subject. Having left the mother's body, the male subject transforms his desire to find a home, an object into a repression of a maternal space. In this fantasy the house becomes the mother's body. However this fantasy, this repression, is put at risk through migrations. The signification of protection translates into one of struggle against internal and external forces: the migrant builds his own version of home/mother/land in an alien and hostile territory where "mother" must be protected in order to be able to offer her own protection. Migration has triggered a recognition of the impossibility of full separation from the "mother" that enables the differentiation between subject and object.

To return to the question, what drives this "wall of war" architecture? It is necessary to reemphasize that while migration entails the crossing of geographic boundaries, its effect is the blurring of boundaries between subject and object. The defensive position in the architecture of eagles and lions is an attempt to protect the home as in traditional war. Such attempts might be considered archaic in the face of recent terrorist attacks that know no sacred space and reveal the home to be not immune to destructive forces—external or internal. What does the mother inscribed onto a defensive

31. See Gaston Bachelard, *The Poetics of Space*, trans. Maria Jolas (Boston: Beacon Press, 1969), and Mieke Bal, *Death and Dissymmetry: The Politics of Coherence in the Book of Judges* (Chicago: University of Chicago Press, 1988) for an elaboration of this masculine fantasy.

architecture signify? Historically feminine spaces such as the home have been transformed into major institutions of resistance. The home has been the site of political resistance in the form of meeting places, hiding places, bomb factories, and escape hatches. From the signifier of passivity and peace, "mother" becomes a signifier of resistance.

The image of territoriality of the *kyka*[32] marks a particular response in the hegemonic culture because it marks its limit of homogeneity. It records both the point of its (impossible) recognition of difference and, therefore, the position of instability of its "host" subject. In the face of the migrant house, disgust draws the individual host subject into an abyss at the borders of the subject's existence, into the space of the abject. Ironically, in doing what they are meant to do—building a house—migrants do not guarantee assimilation. Signs of cultural difference are produced by and through the most "normal" processes of house building and homemaking. And for the migrant, while "fear cements his compound, conjoined to another world. . . . What he has swallowed up instead of maternal love is an emptiness, or rather a maternal hatred, without a word for the words of the father."[33] For those who inhabit a new cultural order the "original" name and law of the father is unlegitimized—the father no longer has a preestablished access to the symbolic order. The mother inscribed onto the architecture of the house is an empty shell; there is no nurturing mother inside or a father to give the word that will help the migrant resolve this abject mess.

In this situation images of territoriality belie the ambiguity of boundaries, the space of the abject, and the constant shuttling that it enforces between the body and the house, between space and language. While the house has an image of territoriality via its perimeter boundary walls, its scale, its orderliness, and its presence, it marks the instability of borderlines between host and migrant. Words and houses are beings in themselves, beings in the making, prior to becoming "proper" names and "proper" places of things. They speak of unstable identities of both host and migrant, and they mark the site of the difficult relationship between spatiality and language.

It is irony, however, that keeps the abject at bay for the migrant. The narrative about war seems grandiose and of an epic genre that has long been dated. These examples are, after all, stereotypical; not every migrant house is of this architectural configuration. It only takes one peculiar example to dissolve grandiose narratives of war.

32. While this word means "house" my use of the original Macedonian in this text suggests the untranslatability of cultural resonances in this context; it is a term of incommensurability between languages.

33. Kristeva, *Powers of Horror*, 6.

4
Menagerie: smooth
space

One migrant house contains, quietly and humbly, a menagerie of ornamental dogs, donkeys, and giraffes shaded under a tree just beyond the gateways of eagles and the barred fence (fig. 4). Such playful parodies shatter any fixed notions of who can speak and notions of spatial territorialities; they take flight into the smooth spaces of possibility, multiplicity, and heterogeneity.[34]

The migrant is infantilized in different ways by the hegemonic culture.[35] The *kyka* as a site of abjection for the hegemonic culture is in turn dismissed as an "improper" house, an improper object. It insists that migrants, like children, do not know what they want. In Kristeva's theory of the abject a distinction is made between "want," which is a condition of the abject, and "desire," which is always for an object. Kristeva argues that the experience of want precedes those of desire and subjectivity; it is the experience on which any being, meaning, language, or desire is founded.[36] Migrants buy land and build a house. This is clearly a situation in which the territorial frontiers of the hegemonic culture are negotiated by the migrants. Their desire is clearly constructed in the image of the house as it was, initially, in the image of the city. Berger and Mohr put this desire for a "proper" place into the political context of migrational movements:

> To be underdeveloped is not merely to be robbed or exploited: it is to be held in the grip of an artificial stasis. Underdevelopment not only kills: its essential stagnation denies life and resembles death. The migrant wants to live. It is not poverty alone that forces him to emigrate. Through his own individual effort he tries to achieve the dynamism that is lacking in the situation into which he is born.[37]

My more speculative interest is in the relationship between spatiality and want/desire, which is mediated by the migrant's body. That space is not an object is particularly important in this distinction. Space is a particularly potent and indefinable entity, perhaps threatening and therefore too quickly dismissed in discursive arenas. It is not inert and passive; it is not an object, and therefore cannot be desired in that sense of the term.[38] Spatiality has been construed as the condition for architectural objectification; it is characterized by formlessness requiring an architect to make a form of it. But it is not simply that a form, a house, is constructed, it is how and by whom. Could it be that architects and migrants are driven by a not too dissimilar desire to make something of

34. See Gilles Deleuze and Félix Guattari, "1227: Treatise on Nomadology: The War Machine," in *A Thousand Plateaus: Capitalism and Schizophrenia*, trans. Brian Massumi (Minneapolis: University of Minneapolis Press, 1987).
35. See Gunew, "Feminism and Politics," 14.
36. Kristeva, *Powers of Horror*, 5.
37. Berger and Mohr, *Seventh Man*, 32.
38. Henri Lefebvre's *The Production of Space* (Oxford: Blackwell, 1991) has most directly tackled the complexities of the theorization of space. The text is critical of the modes in which explorations of space result in some reductionist theory that is either an abstraction into mathematical formulations, a codification into linguistic theories, or an aestheticization into surface treatments.

space? While migration has triggered a modality of abjection characterized by the processes of "rejecting, separating, repeating, abjecting," the potential of spatiality might turn towards "a resurrection that has gone through death (of the ego). It is an alchemy that transforms death drive into a start of life, of new significance."[39] It is an opportunity to give articulation to space and to keep the abject at bay, momentarily or permanently.

The image of territoriality is marked in the metaphoric inscriptions of the mother(land) most often onto the architecture of the *kyka* by the male migrant. The migrant house is characterized by a solidity and a form that has the effect of substitution for the mother(land). As metaphor it also signifies the desire to have access to the symbolic order of the ideal city and the dream house. It is however a house, and to have a "proper" house is to put at risk the "host/guest" structuring that operates on mythic levels. But is this house "proper"? Why not? Metaphoric substitutions are the alien objects that produce the space of the "split subject," which is uncoverable. While the migrant is some sort of doubly split subject, the "host" is also a split subject with a history of migration. But the symbolic order of the host culture is transported transglobally through the use of English as the official language.[40] The migrant house can return the host culture to its own scenes of colonization and nostalgia. But as Gunew argues, because these sites are not always images of England or Ireland, they can produce returns that are uncanny for the host, familiar yet strange renditions of their origin.[41] Thus in the context of this second-level migration there is an unfamiliar sliding of symbolic orders. Perhaps at times they coexist heterogeneously and momentarily as blurred boundaries between "proper" and "improper," between "host" and "migrant." Metaphors are the means by which the split subject is able to enter the symbolic order, and the migrant house is a metaphor. It serves to bridge the splits that reappear continually, but it is also an architectural trace. It is an imaginary bridge— between the here and the elsewhere that is precariously held in tension within an economy of colonized territories, sovereign subjects, and hegemonic cultures.

Vnatre BHatpe

Because of the house's defensive enclosure, its interior space might be thought to be a somewhat protected environment. The interior is historically a signifier of femininity. Within the interiority of the migrant house, femininity is signified by

39. Kristeva, *Powers of Horror*, 15.
40. This is why Sneja Gunew emphasizes that, strictly speaking, Australia can only be termed a postcolonial culture in relation to Aboriginal groups, and to all those "other" migrants different delineations might be more constructive.
41. Gunew, "PMT," 43.

metonymic eruptions of the mother(land); the old culture erupts texturally as ornament. The surfaces of walls, floors, and furnishings are veiled with a myriad of thin coatings—embroideries, lace, photographs, books, cloths, mirrors, souvenirs (figs. 5 and 6). Shiny technological objects are beside or underneath old memorial belongings: "Consciousness has not assumed its rights and transformed into signifiers those fluid demarcations of yet unstable territories . . . there is an effervescence of object and sign—not of desire but of intolerable significance."[42] Metonymic eruptions give the interior space over to the possibilities of becoming. They have a fluid consistency that creates possibilities of difference and of provisional identities that are in a continuous process of resolution. Through attempting to preserve and maintain the mother as signifier of the old symbolic system the interior becomes temporarily and spasmodically a space of the abject—a potential site for a proliferation of fragmented identities. But it is also a space that precedes signifiable things, which nonetheless are significant; it is an effect and not yet a sign. The individual dominated by conflicting drives constitutes his or her own territory, but it is a territory that is edged by the abject. It is possible then that the abject is the space of struggle against the mother, and that in this space the want to be released from the hold of a maternal entity is edged with a desperate drive to be her, to not be divided.[43]

What does the mother(land) signify for the female subaltern, also a mother in/of the house? If, as Gunew speculates, the old symbolic order is reattached to the maternal/feminine, "to the female functions: customs, cooking, costumes, and the old tongues,"[44] does the migrant house open different possibilities for the female subaltern? Perhaps abjection is differently lived within the female subject. Perhaps it does not entail the same sort of sporadic rejections and separations because it is always close to her own body. Perhaps it is less unfamiliar. Kristeva states that "the abject is the violence of mourning for an 'object' that has always already been lost. The abject shatters the wall of repression and judgments."[45] While the defensive gesture of the exterior of the migrant house marks out a (delusive) territoriality between the symbolic order (of the hegemonic culture) and the space of the abject, the interior of the migrant house provides a space in which the symbolic order has less strategic positions for territorial claims. The abject attests to the instability of the symbolic function; it is the underside of the symbolic order. The boundaries between spatiality and language are both constructed and blurred within

42. Kristeva, *Powers of Horror*, 11.
43. See Grosz, *Sexual Subversions*, 78. In the space of the migrant house the (m)other, signifier for the other, the motherland, and the mother tongue, is more radically blurred with the social mother and father due to the absence of paternal access into the (phallic) symbolic order.
44. Gunew, "Home and Away," 37.
45. Kristeva, *Powers of Horror*, 15.

the interior space of the *kyka*, and it is these that constitute the space that must be territorialized continuously in order for the symbolic order to sustain itself.

The abject is not an unambiguous condition—layers, veils, envelopes, can so easily bind and engulf the female migrant. They are not merely quaint expressions of another culture, they are an effect of the interior space. Perhaps this is not abject. Perhaps the female migrant is a *bricoleur*, collecting her fragmented identities. But a *bricoleur* is historically one who practices freedom by wandering aimlessly; "she," the female migrant, does not wander so. She brings many of these things from there, from the other place. Laid out before her are signs of her relocations—her ability to relocate from one house to another, from one country to another. She is relocated, yet her body remains enclosed, contained, enveloped. This house is yet another house, on the other side of the world, but still a house, her container. She has always been a migrant, yet she has always been contained.

The interior of the house is a site for the friction of differing conflictual drives. The mother and the daughter are differently positioned in relation to the mother(land), and have different territorial needs within the metonymic inscriptions of the interior of the *kyka*. Luce Irigaray has elaborated that the specific problem for the mother-daughter relation is marked by fusion/confusion. She suggests a different economy for the relation "in which the two (mother and daughter) are not *identified* in a movement of metaphoric substitution, but *contiguous*: they touch, or associate, or combine."[46] I speculate that within the migrant house "touching" can be either fusional, frictional, or slippery, and that one possibility is that the daughter either removes the metonymic inscriptions or she alters their configuration in an effort to not merely repeat the journey of her mother, but also to not completely cut association, which would amount to a violation of her own subjectivity.

The interior is the site for the secret language of the family, the space for the other language that is identified as a "mother tongue" in relation to the hegemonic culture. It is important to note that the national "phallic" culture constructs these other languages as "mother tongues," although they are actually the first "father's" language.[47] The architecture of the *kyka* is an enclosure. It encloses a space in which the unspeakable is uttered. The migrant house creates a space in which the migrant can speak. But which language? It is not a space in which one can speak to the hegemonic culture, for the

118   46. Luce Irigaray, cited in Margaret Whitford, *Luce Irigaray: Philosophy in the Feminine* (London: Routledge, 1991), 180.
47. This division is not so clear either. The status of languages are globally and historically hierarchized. For example French and German are "more" legitimate than say, Turkish or Maltese. My focus is on the Macedonian language, which has a further construction as an unspeakable mother tongue because of its insecurity in terms of global recognition as a legitimate ethnicity and nation.

migrant is not born into a symbolic order in which the mother tongue is the father's language. The daughter cannot move with ease into the public arena of signs. Let me dwell though on the interiority of the migrant house as a space of becoming for the female migrant. Within the *kyka* is the possibility of a double language, the first father's language and the father's language, and the dangerous slippage from one to the other. It is the interiority of the migrant house that is contiguous with the unspeakable, and both of these are denoted as maternal/feminine. The mother tongue is not the father's language. It is therefore a language that utters the unspeakable and unsignifiable—not signs of objects of desire, but "a wellspring of sign for a non-object."[48] Gunew asks, "What does one do with a nameless power which has the power not to name (the repertoire of the non-verbal) and yet also gives birth to new, arbitrary names?"[49] In defining the abject Kristeva articulates two ways that this repertoire of the nonverbal could go: the symptom is a language that gives up, the subject is inhabited by an alien in its internal structure; sublimation is

> the possibility of naming of the pre-nominal, the pre-objectal, which are in fact only a trans-nominal, a trans-objectal. In the symptom the abject permeates me, I become abject. Through sublimation, I keep it under control. The abject is edged with the sublime. It is not the same moment on the journey, but the same subject and speech bring them into being.[50]

It is important to note this potential in the space of the abject. Within the migrant house, there is always the possibility of giving up speaking and there is also the potential to speak in the modality of the sublime. However, my speculation is that particular individuals within the migrant house are positioned differently in relation to this potential and also that the two possibilities are never fixed; rather they are in constant tension that requires a constant making and remaking of the possibility of becoming a (female subaltern) subject.

The architecture of the *kyka*, thus, in an unplanned and undesigned way,[51] is an inscription of a space for a secret language, a secret knowledge, a mother tongue that coexists with the father's language coming from the outside. It is a space in which the father's language only gains access in a modality, as though it were territorializing a maternal, deterritorialized space. Perhaps it is perceived by the first father as a rape that is a metonymic celebration of territorial acquisition. Perhaps it is for this reason that fathers

48. Kristeva, *Powers of Horror*, 11.
49. Gunew, "Mother Tongue and Migration," 106.
50. Kristeva, *Powers of Horror*, 11.
51. This description is from the perspective of architecture designed by an architect.

tend to frequently "give up" on language as a radical loss (of the mother).[52] Gunew notes that daughters have to witness the humiliation of the first father, and to move from the mother tongue to the father's language means to court new fathers.[53] In relation to the father's language then the mother tongue is constructed as the unspeakable language of guilt. It is a secret language and a secret power; it is a transgression of the language of the symbolic order, the new father's language into which the migrant subject was not born. The site of the *kyka* is therefore a transgressive space. From the position of the (instability) of the host culture it has to be rendered as corrupt or criminal in its socialized appearance. Kristeva states that "an unshakable adherence to Prohibition and Law is necessary if that perverse interspace of abjection is to be hemmed in and thrust aside."[54]

But what of the real mother in the interior? What of the mother's desire? What effects does the migrant house as a space for the mother tongue have on the mother's desire? A number of female theorists have recognized that signs of sexual difference are collapsed into the question of maternity. If the interiority of the migrant house signifies a space of metonymic inscriptions of maternality, what femininities are possible? Is mother also a woman? Is mother as receptacle of the mother tongue the one that speaks? Is the presence of mothering inscribed onto the architecture of the house, which means that the mother is not there to desire or to mother, or to protect her daughter—she works, she is displaced?[55] In order to trace the (im)possible mother's desire I quote Jean Hess, "When I entered these homes I always felt embraced by a room, just as I was often embraced by the woman who had invited me inside."[56]

Hess is describing her personal entry into domestic interiors of northern Mexico, and yet her text is one among many displacements describing the relationship between white women and the female subaltern. The female subaltern is an overdetermined signifier for the mother; the house as maternal space that welcomes back the white woman in its embrace articulates the inscriptions of the mother's body onto the architecture of the house. These displacements engulf the mother in the lace of her own making, in her own metonymic versions of mother(land), in the final product, the (un)finished interior of the house. But what about the mother? She cooks, she works, she makes love, she cleans, she does not stop talking. In the following descriptions of "mother" Gunew suggests a different figure,

52. This of course depends on the particular language that constitutes the mother tongue, the language that is the precondition for one's entry into the symbolic order. However, the rendering of the first fathers as subalterns that have "given up" is most noticeable among the aboriginal peoples of Australia.
53. Gunew, "Mother Tongue and Migration," 106.
54. Kristeva, *Powers of Horror*, 16.
55. For an insightful elaboration of the mother inscribed onto the architecture of house and therefore not present to protect her daughter from the father see chapter 6, "The Architecture of Unhomeliness," in Mieke Bal, *Death and Dissymmetry*.
56. Jean Hess, "Domestic Interiors in Northern New Mexico," *Heresies: A Feminist Publication on Art and Politics*, vol. 3, no. 3, issue 11 (1981): 30.

suddenly small and worn out, and remember nostalgically the energy, the stream of inventiveness which adjusted our balance to the alien fog pressing against the window. Recall too the sudden mysterious raging eruptions. *The mother's thwarted desire....* She always worked; her salary on which the family survived was seen as supplementary. I do not recall the mother tongue other than in that first father's language she gave me, laboriously. No wonder that for me it remained a secret reserve.[57]

As this text also suggests, a mother-daughter relationship is mediated by migration. If "the mother-daughter relationship is the *dark continent* of the *dark continent*,"[58] as Irigaray claims, how dark is the continent of the mother-daughter relationship within the migrant house? Irigaray's statement exemplifies the most significant absence in the symbolic: representation of a maternal genealogy. The mother-daughter relationship is recognized as unsymbolized. It is said that women suffer from an inability to individuate themselves, from a confusion of identity between themselves. If the interiority of the migrant house is the site of abjection, and the space of the mother tongue in which the old symbolic order is reattached to feminine functions, what are the possibilities for women who are always already unrepresentable, unsymbolized? What are the possibilities for the female subaltern to speak? What are the possibilities for the mother and daughter to differentiate in order to speak to one another as women? What modalities of abjection operate within the mother-daughter relationship? If the already blurred boundaries between mother and daughter are negotiated within an abjection mediated by migration, is it the real social mother (also signifier of motherland) by which the daughter is possessed? Kristeva states,

> I experience abjection only if an Other has settled in place and stead of what will be "me." Not at all an other with whom I identify and incorporate, but an Other who precedes and possesses me, and through such possession causes me to be. A possession previous to my advent.[59]

There is no father to give the word to enter the symbolic order, but was there anyhow for the daughter?[60] In the interiority of the migrant house the daughter chokes on the "stuff of love," not only food, but words also, literally the mother tongue, that is offered by her mother and father. She chokes in order to separate from them, " 'I' want none of that element, sign of their desire; 'I' do not want to listen. 'I' do not assimilate. 'I' expel it."[61]

121   57. Sneja Gunew, "The Mother Tongue and Migration," *Australian Feminist Studies* vol. 1, no. 1 (1985): 107.
58. Luce Irigaray, cited in Whitford, *Luce Irigaray*, 77.
59. Kristeva, *Powers of Horror*, 10.
60. My premise is that the daughter's relation to the father/phallus is different to the son's relation to them.
61. Ibid., 3.

In refusing the mother tongue, the daughter refuses everything—her father, especially her mother, and also the motherland—but in such a way that it is ultimately herself that she refuses. And yet within the migrant house, within the space of abjection, there is also a potential for becoming, "during the course in which 'I' become, I give birth to myself amid the violence of sobs, of vomit."[62]

Woman's problem in relation to desire and to subjectivity has been described as a banishment from primary metaphor making, "she can never accomplish the work of mourning the loss of the object (separation from the mother), because she has *no representation of what has been lost.*"[63] For the female migrant—mother or daughter—the motherland might become an object of the loss of the mother. Metonymic practices within the migrant house produce a space/place of mourning. The house becomes tomb or museum, but only as a continually practiced place of cleaning, remaking, mourning. It is however a tomb without a body. For the mother, separation from the motherland might appear as the most fragile and archaic form of abjection. For the maternal-female migrant there cannot be only one division, one separation: "Why? Perhaps because of maternal anguish, unable to be satiated within the encompassing symbolic."[64] The symbolic order is preexisting not only in terms of a paternal lineage in which she is uprooted[65] and relocated, but in terms of global economies in which her husband is also uprooted and relocated. Cleaning and dressing the interior—which is also metonymically the mother-land, which is also signifier of mother—means that the mother can mourn. But that mourning is repeated, rejected. The maternal anguish of the female migrant? Rage, loss, abjection.

Separate rooms and a passage constitute divisions within the migrant house. Outbuildings comprise the order and division of the external space as well as an archi-tecture of difference. In addition to bedrooms, kitchen, and living room, the migrant house comprises of a number of "production" sites: workshop, garage, sewing room, summer kitchen, shed, vegetable garden. The kitchen is also used in productive ways in addition to preparation of food—study, clothes making, translation, administration, and official correspondence. These delineations are different to those in middle-class houses, in which individual bedrooms are most important in the hierarchy of space. (The children in the migrant house typically share one bedroom.)

62. Kristeva, *Powers of Horror*, 3.
63. Whitford, *Luce Irigaray*, 86.
64. Kristeva, *Powers of Horror*, 12.
65. "Uprooting" is a term that surfaces at Macedonian weddings. At the end of the ceremony a song is sung that is specifically about the separation of daughter from mother: *chereshna od koren korneshe, kerka od majka deleshe.*

Other "productive" sites provide possibilities of different creativities, different bodies. These spaces create the possibility of becoming differently, an economy of consumption is partly resisted by a history of domestic production. They are spaces of production on another level, of making and remaking oneself. For the daughter within the space of the migrant house in which the first father's language is identified as a mother tongue, the mother(land) signifies an absent body of the mother; the loss of the mother is lived closely, intimately, abjectly. Only in a room of her own can the daughter remake herself, and she can only remake herself heterogeneously through the experience of abjection, "which is nevertheless managed by the Other, 'subject' and 'object' push each other away, confront each other, collapse, and start again—inseparable, contaminated, condemned, at the boundary of what is assimilable, thinkable: abject."[66] Only in naming the abject in its layered, woven, ambivalent conflictual flux can she mark out a territory—a territory of signs, objects, and words that establish a distance, a space to keep at bay the dangers of absorption it poses.

The daughter makes territorial claims within the interior of the house. She marks out a space, a "study," in which monitoring the door is a mechanism of control, a mechanism of separation.[67] This space is a "closet" in that it detaches itself from the interior, temporarily, and it is an enclosure in which surfaces a private war between words, between languages. The daughter can make a territorial claim for an immaterial production, for knowledge, in which she practices a double language; as Gunew suggests, she becomes a spy, "she uses her double language and secret knowledges of what lies beyond the surface appearances eventually to rewrite both traditions."[68] The study is the space of private writing. The foreigner in ourselves is sublimated, named, and renamed, and renamed again. The architecture of the house delineates a space for the production of a different symbolic order. The daughter pushes the existing symbolic order to its limits— she incorporates words that are untranslatable, "signifying the indigestible element...lacunae and ellipses [that] undermine the possibility of a universalist discourse."[69]

Mala Majka Makedonija

"A tireless builder, the deject is in short a stray. He is on a journey."[70] If migration entails abjection as a spatial configuration constructed within the migrant house,

123

66. Kristeva, *Powers of Horror*, 18.
67. For a further discussion of the daughter's study see Mirjana Lozanovska, "Excess: A Thesis on [Sexual] Difference and Architecture" (Ph.D. thesis, Deakin University, Victoria, Australia, 1994), chapter 6.
68. Gunew, "Feminism and Politics," 14.
69. Ibid., 15.
70. Kristeva, *Powers of Horror*, 8.

7
Migrant enclave,
Thomastown,
Melbourne

it is understood that the building of the house is an ongoing process, it is never complete because it can never attain a solid (stable) subjectivity.

> For the space that engrosses the deject, the excluded, is never one, nor *homogeneous*, nor *totalizable*, but essentially divisible, foldable, and catastrophic. A devisor of territories, languages, works, the deject never stops demarcating his universe whose fluid confines... constantly question his solidity and impel him to start afresh.[71]

Migrants are productive bodies; they build houses. Migrant enclaves are the result of bodies wanting/desiring space. Within these enclaves they explore the possibilities of speaking differently, of weaving and layering different mother tongues and the father's language with one another.[72] In the enclave migrants can speak among one another.

The migrant enclave is seen to be quite monstrous from the perspective of the Anglo-Celtic monoculture in Australia. "Aah yuk!" is the response, sometimes unspoken, to images of so-called "Mediterranean palaces" in Australia (fig. 7). It is an immediate response from the self-named "host culture" that positions itself outside multiculturalism in non-aboriginal Australia. But what lurks behind this response that on the surface seems to be just a typical white middle-class response about aesthetics and good taste, and that seems to be an overdetermined signifier of class, race, and ethnicity? What is unspoken in this response into which so much academic and political effort goes? What are the anxieties of the hegemonic culture?

Kristeva, suggests that oral disgust—"aah yuk"—signifies the abject. As a refusal of the limits of the self it would indicate in this case the refusal of the limit of the host culture and the limit of the individual subject. Kristeva identifies oral disgust as the most archaic form of abjection. One could extrapolate that "aah yuk" as a distinctly nonverbal response signifies that the body has already begun to transgress the boundaries between inside and outside into the space of self-repugnance and abjection.

I want to recount briefly a description by Sneja Gunew of a film produced by Australia's Department of Immigration in the 1950s, *No Strangers Here*. It is set in "Littletown" and narrated by the editor of the town's newspaper. The story begins when he receives several anonymous letters saying that foreigners are not wanted here, signed "A True Australian." As the editor strolls through town he notices the arrival of a foreign

124   71. Ibid., 8.
72. At work in the factories, women learned other "mother tongues" rather than English, the father's language, in order to speak with one another. The factory is yet another architectural site for a study of spatiality and language.

family; although their country of origin is carefully not specified, they are uncannily blonde and good looking. The family rather quickly finds their niche in the town—the father works in the brickwork, the son goes to school, the daughter is an aide in the local hospital, and the mother remains at home, where the editor decides to pay her a visit. He enters her home with the words, "Please tell me the story of your life." On the brink of answering, the mother rushes over to the oven where something more urgent is calling for attention. She offers the editor a slice of homemade cake and he in turn requests the recipe, which is published in the local paper under the heading "Easy to Mix." The mother offers food instead of words. Food in Australia, as we know, is a more digestible way to accept multiculturalism.[73]

Food rather than fluency is what is expected. Words and houses provoke anxieties because they are reminders of the unstable status of the host culture. Architectural productivity, migrants building houses, functions as a mode of resistance, a counterpower against the forces of the hegemonic culture. These houses demonstrate the arbitrariness of the host-migrant dynamic, which makes evident the arbitrariness of power operating in linear and dichotomous center-margin structures. Thus it is evident that power cannot so easily be pinned down, that it operates as a network that flows in many directions and across many nodal points, with potential areas of contradictions: counter-powers.[74] In building their own houses migrants also attest to the complexities in the relations between architecture and power, that architecture can be a pseudo-agent as a mode of resistance, that it is not necessarily the statement of the authority, that it acts against the system while being complicit with it. To the extent that ideologies do not produce space but rather they are in space, the particular ideology of the dream house translated through home ownership in Australia results in a quite different effect with respect to the migrant house—that of threatening the homogeneity the national culture intended. While the threat seems to be one of aesthetics, anxieties that are lurking in the shadows strike at the constitution of culture itself, of knowledge, of language, and of the construction of space, "They spawn ghettos which harbor unspeakable un-Australian crimes and diseases, particularly intellectual ones."[75]

The migrant house represents the site of the abject for the (unstable) subject position of the host culture. The abject is anterior to the subject/object bifurcation.

73. Sneja Gunew, "Against Multiculturalism: Rhetorical Images," *Typereader: Journal of the Centre for Studies in Literary Education* 7 (Autumn 1992): 28–41.
74. See Michel Foucault, *An Introduction*, vol. 1 of *The History of Sexuality*, trans. Robert Hurley (New York: Penguin Books, 1978) for this analysis of power.
75. Gunew, "Against Multiculturalism," 36.

"Abjection is above all ambiguity,"[76] and it is this ambiguity that undoes the neat division between subject/object and host/migrant. The migrant house threatens the homogeneity and hegemony (which are only in fact arbitrary constructions); as the site of abjection, the migrant house is the limit to its (un)stable cultural subjectivity. The architecture of the migrant house constructs a reversal of the function of the tongue between the host culture and the migrant. The host culture responds to the migrant house in aesthetic terms; the *kyka* is an architecture of "bad taste," an entity that leaves an unpleasantness on the tongue. Yet while this mode of response renders the tongue into its mode of speaking, it also renders the tongue into its function of tasting, of consuming. "Bad taste" signifies consumption; it is a mild form of oral disgust. "Abjection signals the frailty of the object as the support of the subject."[77] The host culture cannot speak about the migrant house, it can only (not) digest it. The host culture is brought into a confrontation between itself and the other in a world in which the boundaries are blurred; it chokes on its own limits. The migrant house thus draws the host culture into the field of the abject, threatening it with an "abyss that marks the place of its birth *and* obliteration, posing both an internal and an external threat to its stability."[78] In altering the function of the tongue of the host culture, the migrant house is (not) digested as an offering of "food." The migrant house is not "food" in the literal sense, for while it is not yet words, it is an image, it is an architecture. It is the space of a particular mother tongue, *Majka Makedonija*. Within the migrant house the migrant speaks the unspeakable, a secret language, even a double language, slipping from one to the other. Thus there is a reversal of the function of the tongue: the host culture consumes (and spits out the food); the migrant speaks (utterances of the tongue).

From the perspective of the hegemonic culture, big *kyki* are seen to participate in their own reproduction; autonomously and immaculately (without the father!), they form migrant enclaves. Described as tribes and villages, which ultimately cannot be dismissed, they have the effect of returning the earlier generations to the scene of their own colonial origins, to the scene of colonial nostalgia. As Gunew argues in "Home and Away," a violent uncanniness is released in the realization that while Australia is always a construct that is mediated by somewhere else, the image of the migrant enclave is a reminder that somewhere else is not inevitably always the image of England or Ireland. Within Australia other motherlands erupt as spaces of abjection.

126   76. Grosz, "Language and Limits," 109.
           77. Ibid.
           78. Ibid., 110.

Abjection in the context of the migrant enclave opens possibilities for eruptions of mother tongues, of utterances that in an uncanny mode incorporate the other, the foreigner in ourselves within the symbolic order. At a second level abjection the migrant enclave signifies for the host culture a muteness and a debt owed to the maternal space(s). Elizabeth Grosz notes a general disinterest in psychoanalytic theory (and in linguistic theories inspired by these) in the details of the pre-Oedipal phases. Even in the most complex theories of the "split subject" the focus is on the already "resolved" subject, the subject that is already socialized and "Oedipalized." These theories tend to ignore the processes of becoming, the conditions and the drives that make it possible for the speaking subject to emerge. Grosz claims that this constitutes a theoretical blind spot that "may well be related to a sociocultural and discursive silence about the relations between the developing social and speaking subject and the *maternal space* sustaining and nourishing it."[79] She argues that this maternal space marks the site of an unspeakable debt of life and existence that both the individual and culture owe to the mother and the maternal body but can never acknowledge, let alone repay. The abject is sited in this maternal space within the preservation of a "pre-objectal" relationship, "in the immemorial violence with which a body becomes separated from another body in order to be."[80]

The "host" culture responds to the migrant enclave with horror, signifying the abject. The abject is a return of the mother, but, as Gunew suggests in "Feminism and Politics," she returns as the devouring mother. Words, utterances from mother tongues, threaten the father language—English can be swallowed up by those most "improper" appropriations, chaotic barbaric mixtures of tongues. The mother returns to devour her offspring. Most threatening are those that can slip from one to the other, from the father's language to the mother tongue, and laugh—the sound of the subaltern that is not yet a sign.

In establishing architectural boundaries the migrant enclave blurs and threatens the boundaries of languages. It constructs spaces in which languages are rendered pluralistic—words from England are mingled with words from *Makedonija*; many words are both and neither. The writing of this essay is itself a practice of recovering the maternal space through architectural space, the migrant house in the New World, and yet it is also a means of keeping the abject at a distance. "Immaculate" is perhaps an apt term in which to describe the migrant landscape. Its hard, shiny, clean surfaces impress an

79. Ibid., 113.
80. Kristeva, *Powers of Horror*, 10.

image of an excessively ordered environment, an environment that attempts to keep at bay the fluidities of the abject. It is evident then that it is not lack of cleanliness and order that causes abjection, but that which "disturbs identity, system, order. What does not respect borders, positions, rules. The in-between, the ambiguous, the composite."[81] It is evident then that it is not the lack of physical borders of the architecture that cause abjection, but the ambiguity of borders between spatiality and language, between visuality and the tongue.

The immaculate image is one extreme. The other is the production of food that can be seen in the vegetable gardens on the embankments of main roads in migrant enclaves; offerings of food are the migrant's only acceptable and legitimate signifiers. The migrant enclave is a pluralistic space, a space of multiplicity, but not before cultural difference, nor before sexual difference. The individual migrant cannot speak to the hegemonic culture—a division is marked and re-marked between citizen and migrant. But the migrant can build and (s)he can produce, (s)he wishes to offer a different body. Bodies are productive, they build houses. "They wish to offer their bodies in a new way, a new language, a new space. New words, new spaces create new bodies."[82] Why does the migrant build? If it is as an effort to enter the symbolic order, to escape the conditions of stasis and stagnation, it is ironical that the building also constructs an architecture of abjection. The architecture of the migrant house and the migrant enclave constructs an illegitimate and disavowed maternal space in which the possibility of mother tongues and plurality of words also keeps the migrant bodies within the space of abjection. They cannot speak to the hegemonic culture. While the bodies are ceaselessly productive, they are simultaneously burnt out; they are perhaps the sites of patriarchal sacrifice, a sacrifice in a world in which the (m)other has collapsed and yet cannot be altogether removed, a payment for the "umbilical debt" owed by the individual and society. The architecture however survives as the trace of a subjectivity-in-the-process-of-becoming.

In producing an architectural frontier the *kyka* induces the dismantling of the boundaries between languages. The migrant has constructed a wall. On one side of the wall the hegemonic culture responds with oral disgust; words are spat out, the other is repelled, a sign of abjection. On the other side, each family member struggles with a particular role in relation to the (m)other; some recreate and repeat the other, while others keep the abject at bay, new words are invented, a double language is at play. In the former

81. Ibid., 4.
      82. Gunew, "Against Multiculturalism," 31.

situation, the migrant's territorial claims render spatiality as signifier of the abject in relation to the language of the hegemonic culture. In the latter situation spatiality within the architectural frontier is the site of becoming a subject (a social, speaking being) and a (spatially) embodied being. In this sense the migrant house is the spatial (pre)condition for the production of a different subjectivity, or rather a subjectivity in which difference proliferates. It is the spatial (pre)condition for the (secret) dismantling of the hegemony of one language. Spatiality is potentially a site in and through which mother tongues can proliferate. To recognize the potency in the relation between spatiality and the tongue is to put the primacy of visuality in architecture and urbanism at quite some risk. The unspeakable and the "unsignifiable" in architecture is that it not only matters what the architecture looks like but that architecture is intricately entangled with culture and language and that it "improperly" constructs the possibility of multiple speaking positions. Visuality is a pretense about aesthetic distance that is ironically turned inside out in the exclamation of oral disgust.

This silence in architectural discourse can perhaps be represented (simplistically) as the mute term in the discourse on architectural form, namely the term "space." Form is prevalent and central, lending itself to the criterion of visuality and the safety of the "product" (the resolved subject); space as the site of possible becoming is silenced. Space is aligned with the body as the precondition for form; it is the site of its birth and its obliteration. It is the mute term because at any moment it might erupt—it has the potency to speak rather than to be seen.

In warding off these (non)unsightly spaces, the hegemonic culture wards of the unnamable: the mother tongues are suppressed within the *kyki*, within the migrant enclaves. However, as Kristeva asserts in relation to her theory of abjection, "what is excluded can never be fully obliterated but hovers at the borders of our existence."[83] The migrant house as the site of abjection blurs the boundaries between wall and space, subject and object, citizen and migrant. *Kyki* disturb identity, system, and order, respecting no definite positions, rules, boundaries, or limits of culture and language. They can threaten the apparent unity of the host subjectivities with disruption and dissolution. The migrant enclaves represent the limit of the unity of the hegemonic culture. Abjection is what the symbolic order must reject, cover over, or contain. The abject in turn beckons the host culture ever closer to its edge.

83. Grosz, "Language and Limits," 108.

Cacophony: Gratification or Innovation
Wong Chong Thai

Over recent years, unparalleled economic prosperity has dramatically altered Pacific Rim cities. Where the social and physical landscape once resonated with overtones from Somerset Maugham's *East of Suez* or George Orwell's *Burmese Days*, the present dominance of international capital has virtually erased most attributes of the previous landscape and its spatial and social contingencies. In the days of the empire the spatial landscape was formed with an imperial gaze in mind. Indigenous and colonial quarters were clearly demarcated, and entry into the other's terrain came with varying degrees of violence, fascination, and disgust. Traditional bungalows with their verandahs, the European clubhouse (described by Orwell as the real seat of British power and the town center), and the church were contrasted by the native quarters with their bazaars. Merchandise and artifacts of the East and the West adorned these spaces simultaneously. Lancashire-made cotton shirts and incredibly cheap German clocks were displayed adjacent to locally made glazed earthenware jars, lacquered sandals, chickens cheeping in wicker cages, brass Buddhas, alligator hide with magical properties, and the like. The stench, the din, and the nameless and faceless crowd did not go unnoticed. Together with the enervating, humid, tropical climate, they made the clubhouse a place of refuge and congregation for the Europeans.

Even now, when electronic communications, global trade, international finance, and ever-easier travel have compressed time and space sufficiently for East and West to experience a closeness never before felt, fascination for the other(s) still emerges to incite an imagination of unease and admiration. In several recent articles, Fredric Jameson was sufficiently intrigued by the East Asian region, mainly Japan and China, to construct a theory of future space, space that Jameson has described as "dirty realism" and "compensatory space."[1] His encounters with the East evoked an anxiety that is very much like America's former obsession with the Soviet Union or Elizabethan England's vision of Spain. No doubt, China's unprecedented economic growth and affluence, and the accompanying spatial and social changes, prompted Jameson to express his discomfort. For him, the enrichment of the peasantry will enable a rapid form of development that will

1. Fredric Jameson, "Demographies of the Anonymous," in *Anyone*, ed. Cynthia Davidson (New York: Rizzoli, 1991), 56–57.

alter the landscape in a random fashion. The ensuing ensembles, in his view, will be like meteorites, randomly placed, fixed more by their falls than by some logic or necessity. The proliferation of buildings and infrastructural development of all kinds, together with the affluence and seemingly wanton consumption in China, has moved Jameson to reverse the notion of dystopia. Where previously the dystopian imagination meant a sort of pessimism (a catastrophe equal to the worst of the bad), the new Chinese landscape is a dystopia of wealth. Jameson finds it hard to imagine a reality of one and one-quarter billion people wantonly consuming and building. The catastrophe befalling unto the earth as a result of such consumption is inconceivable to him.[2]

  This condition led Jameson to think in a Hegelian manner that the despotic Asiatic mode is now the supplement or the "other" to the now defunct and dissolved North American civil society. In his view the Asiatic will be to the Western what the medieval was to the Gothic Revival and the tribal archaic to the Modern.[3] For Jameson, therefore, the collapse of the civil society in the "post-industrial" and "late-capitalist" age suggests the emergence of a new compensatory space—a space that is the geographical other within a landscape of enclaves, each enclave being formed out of a particular group's separatist interest and demand.[4] This form of spatiality, which Jameson claims is the result of a new micropolitics, will materially affect the future of America, if it has not already done so. This compensatory space provides a sense of "no-man's land," absorbing various multiple yet incommensurate subjectivities. And because of the loss resulting from the dissolution of civil society, this compensatory space allows the old bourgeois subject to reimagine and reassume him- or herself. Yet, this space is not to be feared. On the contrary, it is the "space of urban infinite space, where corporate property has somehow abolished the older individual private property without becoming public."[5]

  Jameson further suggests that this compensatory space has the mark of the "obligatory Japanese reference," the great other whose success the West admires and fears at the same time. Rather than render the Japanese challenge as invalid, America has to struggle with and against Japan in order to survive, if not to mount a counteroffensive. In the ensuing struggle, Jameson views Japan as the future's benchmark whose image and reference America needs to compulsively imitate.[6] Hence, the compensatory space, as Jameson would have it, draws heavily from Tokyo:

2. Fredric Jameson, "The Uses of Apocalypse," in *Anyway*, ed. Cynthia Davidson (New York: Rizzoli, 1994), 40–41.
3. Jameson, "Demographies of Anonymous," 57.
4. According to Jameson the old bourgeois self, if it had ever existed in America, is certainly fractured by now. Because of new economical and political contexts, the old class lines are fragmented into a host of small groups: yuppies, the rich and famous, the underclass, and the homeless. "Each group fantasizes the totality of the others as the bourgeois society or the state"; Jameson calls this phenomenon "separatism." These new class lines instill a certain consciousness whereby each group begins to exert a political presence. They also generate a "compensatory" space, however, which allows various groups to lose their identities and to intermingle in historically unprecedented ways. Ibid., 60.

The street is somehow inside, so that the city as a whole, which has no profile, becomes one immense, amorphous, unrepresentable container that realizes the conceptual essence of the geodesic dome. The echo of this macro-phenomenon within, in the parts or micro-structures, does not take place in the hotels but rather in the department stores. In these open emporia one finds food markets, theaters, bookstores, and all kinds of other specialized services run together in a fashion that derives ultimately and historically from the great open-air markets or bazaars of the East and of precapitalist modes of production.[7]

Here, Jameson seems to have located his site of fancy in scenes from the East and the movie *Blade Runner*. The intention of this paper, however, is not to contend with the extent by which fascination and fear produce a "lack" in Jameson. The point is that a fascination and fear that produce a desire that valorizes and appropriates aspects of the East are embodied within the writings of Jameson. One can criticize Jameson to have used the East for an internal critique of the West's own logocentrism. His analyses are specifically directed at late capitalism and the postmodern dissolution of the civil society in the West. This prompts him to view aspects of the East as potentially redemptive spaces for the West to imitate. This logic polarizes the East as the West's other.[8] Furthermore, the Hegelian sublation used in Jameson's formulation leaves the East as a passive force and voice, always to be judged by an authority located elsewhere.

Jameson can be criticized for falling into a binary totality that polarizes imaginary opposites rather than allowing difference to surface. After having identified aspects of Japan as spaces to be imitated, Jameson surreptitiously slips in Rem Koolhaas's works, seeing them as synonymous to the amorphous sprawl of Tokyo. He claims that the rigid, undifferentiated grid of service cores found in Koolhaas's *Delirious New York* enables a spatiality that fosters a randomness, a freedom, and a differentiation found so often in Tokyo.[9] Here, the sprawl of Tokyo seems to have been reduced, condensed, and contained by Koolhaas's grid. Furthermore, the predicate suggests that the East is incoherent, chaotic, and random—a perceived cacophony that makes no sense to the symbolic world. I would argue that despite his reductive notion of Eastern spaces instigated by fear and fascination, Jameson offers the possibility of uncovering and revealing a current cross-

5. Ibid., 56.
6. Ibid., 56.
7. Ibid., 56.
8. Jameson polarizes the "East" by projecting America's future through a process that assimilates elements from Japan. This is based on a historical projection where he sees Japan's and Europe's development lagging behind America's. Jameson may be right in his observation, but in adopting this equation, he renders the "East," or at least Japan, passive. The same tone prevails in the way he speaks about the difference between Arata Isozaki's and Rem Koolhaas's work. See Jameson interviewed by Michael Speaks in "Envelopes and Enclaves: The Space of Post-Civil Society," *Assemblage* 17 (April 1992): 33–35.
9. Ibid., 33.

cultural phenomenon that has material affect on the production of architecture. I am referring to the phenomenon of globalization, which seems to be the absolute opposite of regionalism. For if globalization can be described as an expansion of perspective, then regionalism is an implosion.

Koolhaas's use of the term "globalization" remains vague due to the speculative nature of the essay. Yet he opens up a space that enables me to address this issue in the context of Singapore, if not the Far East. There seem to be significant differences in the operation of "globalization" in different parts of the world. In Europe and America, architectural production is certainly permeated by cross-cultural interpenetrations resulting from migration, media, and other such means. (I do not wish to delve deeply into this issue here.) In America and Europe, globalization, in architectural terms, seems to be highly influenced by technological systems superimposed onto one another. Projects such as Rem Koolhaas's Parc de la Villette and Bernard Tschumi's Kyoto Station and his notions of "techno-bodies," "techno-programs," and "techno-conditions" are some predicates. There is a sleekness in these architects' work, which, when formally analyzed, is expressed as a series of pure surfaces. In the "East," on the other hand, cross-cultural imports are constantly being disturbed by traces of the natives' uncanny past; primitivism, barbarism, etc. Therefore, in the globalization process in the East, the affects of modernity are not only being enacted after the fact but also, in one way or another, intruded by traces of the (pre)colonial past. These excesses take more the form of the material and the corporeal than the "mechanical" and the "technological."[10]

What then is this chaotic space in the East? And how may it offer itself as a critical practice within the present forms of production and knowledge? To answer these questions, one might interpret Jameson's concept of the amorphous, the random, and the chaotic as implying a diversity of disjunctive parts that appear and disappear, condense and disperse over time and space. And if such spaces offer critical possibilities to rethink received notions of architecture, they may also offer a place where subjectivities themselves undergo reflections whereby they can be emptied and denied.

To excavate and extend the notions of chaos, randomness, and amorphousness in the East, Gilles Deleuze's interpretation of Gottfried Wilhelm Leibniz proves helpful. As Deleuze puts it,

10. See Rem Koolhaas, "Architecture and Globalization," *GSD News* (Winter/Spring 1994): 47–48.

1
Expressway slicing
between blocks,
Causeway Bay,
Hong Kong

Chaos would be the sum of all possibles, that is, all individual essences insofar as each tends to existence on its own account; but the screen only allows compossibles—and only the best combination of compossibles—to be sifted through.[11]

Singularities and possibles, according to him, are never constant, consistent, and stable but are capable of extension, alteration, and disconnection in varied ways and intensities. And although they may suddenly discontinue in flight, they nevertheless strive to exist in their autonomous state or in their concomitant mix, which is always in a constant state of flux.[12] Only through this process, Deleuze claims, can permanence emerge from chaos. Singularities and possibles crisscross among themselves without any predefined route, direction, or end. Where their paths meet, new trajectories may be formed to take new paths and directions. Each, like events, permit new possibilities, creations, and inventions. They strive to take us to new frontiers and unexplored terrains.[13] Referring to Leibniz's notion of the monad, Deleuze states that apprehended possibles are the coming together or the dispersal of various series of singularities and possibles either within the monad or within the world.[14]

At this stage, these apprehended possibles appear and disappear with or without any form of regularity and synchrony. Their emergence as possibles are conceivable only because they are chosen from an infinity of possible worlds. The existing world can be considered relatively the "best."[15] As Deleuze quotes Leibniz, "God chooses between an infinity of possible worlds incompossible with each other and chooses the best." Here all questions of causality are rendered irrelevant. As Leibniz stated "everything that happens has a reason" and that provides sufficient explanation.[16] If the existing world with all its compossibilities is relatively the best, then, for our purposes, the convergence and divergence of the series of singularities and events that make up the compossibilities cannot be based on some reflection and intimation from a more profound and eternal absolute world.[17] The latter, though perfect, is nevertheless external and is therefore always imaginary.

Deleuze's analysis proves useful to reinterpret Jameson's explanation of the urbanscape in the East. One may say, for example, that the access way slicing in close proximity between two city blocks from an expressway into dense Hong Kong (fig. 1), when

11. Gilles Deleuze, *The Fold: Leibniz and the Baroque,* trans. Tom Conley (Minnesota: University of Minneapolis Press, 1988), 77.

12. Ibid., 79.

13. The seemingly aleatory nature of this phenomenon is not analogous to the throw of a dice. Leibniz believes that the perceived arbitrariness of the process is the result of our incapacity to discern the various flights within a depthless shadow. Trajectories take flight depending on principles of convergence and divergence. It is only by multiplying events and allowing more collisions that one can begin to invent orders and principles. See Deleuze, *The Fold,* 66.

14. Ibid., 76–77.

15. Ibid., 60.

2
Street scene,
Ueno, Tokyo

3
Shopfronts,
Causeway Bay,
Hong Kong

measured against some eternal perfect world, may seem improbable. Perceived within that particular moment and context of Hong Kong however, it is the best possible. Or, for that matter, the existing gamut and the confusion of signs in competition, as found in the Ueno and Shibuya districts in Tokyo and in Hong Kong, can be accepted as the best possible installments for the present context (figs. 2 and 3). The contradictions and the schisms between billboards and street-front transparencies, vending machines and traditional banners, English and Japanese terms, and Sumo wrestlers and Hollywood actors are made equivalent. They are compossible. Their existing mix and composition for that particular moment can be acknowledged as "the best." No doubt some of the graphics and ideas can be traced to some moment in the past. Yet their present state is never fixed and certain. The conditions of tomorrow may differ from that of the present. Hence, the signs may consolidate and replicate a thousandfold, disperse and disappear only to reappear in other forms. They coexist for reasons that escape us, very much like the appealing but yet unsettling contradictions of Zen monks in Kyoto who wear Nike shoes and Georgio Armani sunglasses, ride motorcycles, and spend their evenings watching television game shows.

These anachronisms, differences, and incommensurabilities in their state of flux overlap, diminish, and dissolve not only the seams that divide them but the very architecture that contains them. For these happenings recognize no limits and no traces of any hierarchy in their architecture. One such site of this state of flux is the food court, with its diversity of food outlets. "Junction 8" in Singapore, for example, features fast-food sushi, Swenson's ice cream, meatballs with noodles, and other specialties. The differences and similarities between their settings, though apprehended, cannot be easily identified. The outlet for Swenson's, an American ice cream chain, is rendered similar to the stalls of local food by such features as the wood veneer finish of its counter front and the checkered tiled background wall. The identity of each stall is made perceivable only by the subtle differences between their technologies, their signs, and a few special features. In the case of Swenson's, signature lamps and a special neon sign replace those that front the neighboring stalls.

The sushi and teppan-yaki stalls are more sufficiently differentiated, however, probably because of the form of service and the technology involved. At the sushi bar, the sushi are conveyed by a powered toy train. Diners pick their favorite combinations

16. Gottfried Wilhelm Leibniz, cited in ibid., 41.

17. On Deleuze's notion of eternity see Conley's introduction in ibid., 79. Conley states that Deleuze, though a utopian, does not merely ground his theories to a "no where" but to the "now here" wherever the concept of space is taken up.

4
Food court,
Junction 8,
Bishan, Singapore

from the conveyor belt and are charged subsequently. The teppan-yaki stall, on the other hand, is a transformed version of the Japanese model. Here, counter-seated diners are served directly from the gas-fired iron frying plate (fig. 4). The stir-fried dishes are simplified eclectic versions of Chinese food tailored to the Singapore appetite. There is less orchestration in the frying, lighting, and seating. The entire outlet is designed for immediacy. Unlike the teppan-yakis found in Japanese restaurants, those here do not allow privacy and relaxation. In any case, who will notice and demand such differences?

In Junction 8, one may talk about other modes of difference as well. The ceiling, for example, is demarcated by the "high-tech" look of exposed metal pipes in one area and a suspended wooden ply in another. The former speaks of the machine while the latter of craft. Yet, the furniture in each area does not complement the space that it serves. The "bentwood" chairs would under "normal" circumstances be placed under the suspended wooden ceiling and the "Philippe Starck" seats would be compatible with the high-tech look. Under a cacophonic setting, however, where even the in-house music churns out English, Chinese, and Japanese tunes with a regularity beyond comprehension, such complementation seems redundant in a spatial practice whose hierarchies are confusing to say the least.

Obviously the description of these cacophonic tones cannot sufficiently capture the simultaneous happenings in that space. There are other collisions such as the multiplicity of floor finishes, the realist wall murals of quaint townscapes and people, and various signs featuring Chinese and roman characters. Added to the scene are the people who fill the intervening space; ever changing in volume; waiting, queuing, and eating; all engrossed in their own specific activities. Finally, the simultaneous presence of technology and corporate culture form the backdrop. The former is emphasized by the use of such elements as an air-conditioning and ventilating system, a sprinkler, and security devices. The latter can be felt through the cleanliness and the hygiene of the place, and the different uniforms of the staff resulting from their specific job functions.

In Junction 8, in the midst of celebrating diversity and multiplicity, one experiences an intensity that frustrates any hope of access to some form of authenticity and history. Reality seems flattened; things of the past are made contemporaneous with the present. Myth seems to have been extended into fact. English terms exchange value with

5
Display of skinned
chickens at a
chicken-and-rice
stall, Pasir Ris
Coffee Shop,
Singapore

other, more archaic, and, at times, impermeable signs. These phenomena occur with a velocity that results in transience. In all this flatness, flashbacks of archaic pasts and estrangements occur with unpredictable frequency, which tends to dissolve and discredit notions of hierarchy, geometry, models, and genealogy customarily projected by architecture. They "empty" the received practices and ideologies of architecture. The old, valued compositions and hierarchies are turned around and, at times, robbed of their accepted meanings. The dissolution of formal and compositional attributes operates very much like the display of a chicken-and-rice stall in which countless grotesque chickens exceed the very thing that contains them (fig. 5). Architecture emerges from the shadowy darkness of chaos to reassert itself. Therefore, chaos is not necessarily random. It may be organized with its own grid and logic, which may have a chance to surface in Junction 8 and other similar spaces.

However, this is unlike Koolhaas's grid imposed onto an undifferentiated mass. We therefore need to turn Jameson's earlier assertion around. Koolhaas's grid, instead of opposing the active force of chaos (which Jameson associates with the East), exemplifies Koolhaas's failure to prevent chaos from taking over. Indeed, this may have been his intention.[18] In this way, the grid becomes a cog in the chaotic Asian machine. Differences between the grid and chaos can, at some levels, become seemingly seamless, whereby chaos subsequently absorbs and overcomes the grid to reduce it into one member in the sum of all possibles. Hence, architecture resumes the aleatory convergence of some singularities where they subsequently emerge as possibles. Chance, coincidence, accident, and reason bring autonomous singularities together not to reconcile their differences, though such a possibility exists, but to allow a nexus where new possibles and intentions and all implications of some eternal future are deemphasized and replaced by an experimentation and invention for the here and now. To quote Deleuze, "The best of all worlds is not the one that reproduces the eternal, but the one in which new creations are produced, the one endowed with a capacity for innovation or creativity."[19] Here provocations replace mimesis as the basis of any fundamental argument on knowledge and production.

A final word on the subject in such a state of flux. In the chance encounters generated by the new nexus, we are often distanced from our immediate surroundings because of the unfamiliarity resulting from flashbacks and ironies. We are bound to leave

18. In a conversation with Alejandro Zaera Polo, Koolhaas maintains that chaos is inaccessible to architects who can only attempt to prevent it, but fail. It is only in their failure, by accident, that chaos happens. See "OMA/Rem Koolhaas," *El Croquis* 53 (February–March 1992): 5–31. In "Architecture and Globalization" Koolhaas asserts how globalization might finally lead to a definitive discrediting of architecture. I suspect that there is a link for Koolhaas between the notion of chaos and his objective of discrediting architecture—at least the architecture of which we know.
19. Deleuze, *The Fold*, 79.

ourselves and our pasts behind. In a no-man's land, the subject moves freely, unencumbered by the histories carried around at home and in the surroundings of the familiar. Here, we empty our burden of history to take on new possibilities. The very space of Junction 8 then is unlike the retail outlets for such brand names as Levi Strauss, GAP, or Guess. These outlets project ready-made images for East Asia to imitate and consume. The spaces of the Junction 8 food court differ in their insistence on multiplying principles resulting from connections and collisions. And like trajectories in any collision, the denied and emptied bodies are then dispersed to take flight into uncharted and unpredicted territories. Is this then not the new global condition?

Figure Credits

Colquhoun
1, 2. *Ottagono* 98 (March 1991).

Biln
1, 3–8. George Fessy. Published in George Fessy, Jean
Nouvel, and Hubert Tonka, *Institut du Monde Arabe: Une
Architecture de Jean Nouvel, Gilbert Lezénés, Pierre Soria,
Architecture Studio* (Paris: Éditions Champs Vallon, 1988).
2. "Jean Nouvelle," *El Croquis* 65/66 (1994): 68.

Prakash
1, 3, 7. Hasan-Uddin Khan, *Charles Correa* (Singapore:
Concept Media, 1987), 142–43.
2. Willy Boesiger, ed., *Le Corbusier: The Complete
Architectural Works 1952–1957* (London: Thames and
Hudson, 1964), 106.
4. Madhu Khanna, "Space, Time and Nature in Indian
Architecture," *Architecture + Design* (September/October
1991): 58.
5. Vikramaditya Prakash.
6. Adapted from Kulbhushan Jain, "Morphostructure of a
Planned City, Jaipur, India" *Architecture + Urbanism* (August
1978): 108.
8. Satish Grover, "Charles Correa," *Architecture + Design*,
(September/October 1991): 18.

Burns
1, 3. Graphische Sammlung Albertina, Vienna.
2. L. Bakalowits after Adolf Loos, published in Panayotis
Tournikiotis, *Adolf Loos* (New York: Princeton Architectural
Press, 1994), 100–01.
4. Bryan Hammond Collection. Bryan Hammond and Patrick
O'Connor, *Josephine Baker* (Boston: Little, Brown, 1988), 105.

Cairns
1. Jacques Dumarcay, *The House in South-East Asia*, trans.
and ed. Michael Smithies (Singapore: Oxford University Press,
1987), 44.
2–6. Stephen Cairns.

Nalbantoğlu
1. Murat E. Gülyaz and Irfan Ölmez, *Cappadocia* (Nevsehir:
Dünya Turizm, 1994), 15.
2. Burhan Arif, "Köy Projesi" (Project for a village), *Arkitekt*
11–12 (1935): 320.
3. Abdullah Ziya, "Köy Mimarisi" (Village architecture), *Ülkü*
vol. 1, no. 5 (June 1933): 372.
4. Suha Özkan and Selahattin Önür, "Another Thick Wall
Pattern," in *Shelter, Sign and Symbol*, ed. Paul Oliver (London:
Barrie and Jenkins, 1975), 102.
5. Adviye Fenik, "Altindağ Röportajlari" (Altindağ
Interviews), *Zafer*, May 1949.
6. *Ulus*, 5 November 1937, front page.

Lozanovska
All photos by the author.

Wong
All photos by the author.

Colophon

Editing and design
Clare Jacobson

Cover design
Sara Stemen

Special thanks to: Caroline Green, Therese Kelly, Mark
Lamster, and Anne Nitschke of Princeton Architectural
Press—Kevin C. Lippert, publisher

Typography
New Caledonia and Trade Gothic

Printing
Data Reproductions

Paper
Finch Opaque